W9-BDD-357

GRAND RAPIDS CHAPTER
LA LECHE LEAGUE 942-1140

THE GROWING FAMILY SERIES

The Fussy Baby

How to bring out the best in
your high need child

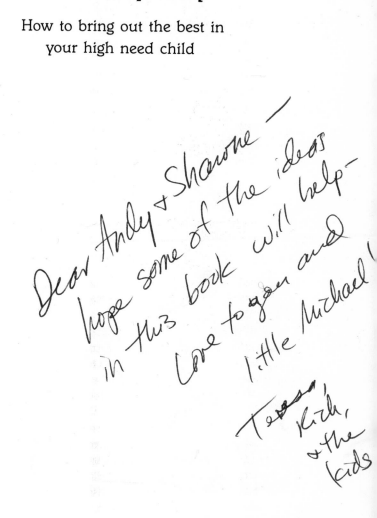

Dear Andy + Sharone —
hope some of the ideas
in this book will help—
Love to you and
little Michael!

Teresa, Rich,
+ the
kids

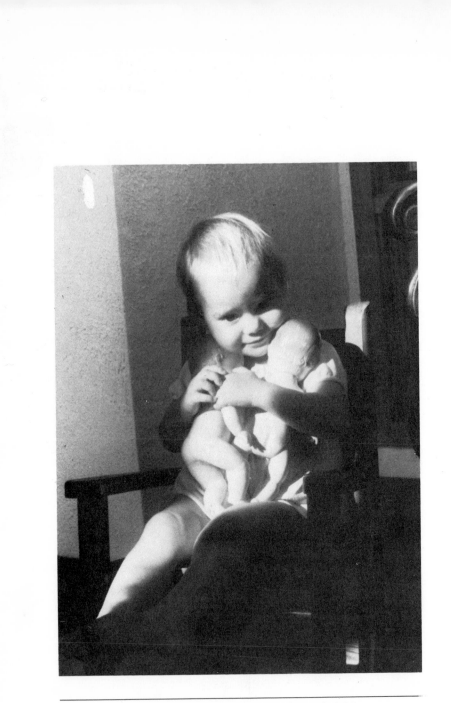

Hayden Sears, the author's high need child

THE GROWING FAMILY SERIES

The Fussy Baby

How to Bring Out the Best in Your High Need Child

William Sears, M.D.

La Leche League International
Franklin Park, Illinois

July 1985
©1985 by William Sears, M.D.
All rights reserved
90 89 88 87 86 85   7 6 5 4 3 2 1

Printed in the United States of America
Photo credits:
  cover, Dale Pfeiffer
  frontispiece, Martha Sears
  p. 38, Harriette Hartigan
  p. 55, Debra Best
  p.87, Sue Buckley
  p. 101, 106, William Sears, M.D.
  p. 104, Mary E. Loewenstein-Anderson
  others, Dale Pfeiffer
Illustrations by Maurice Wagner
Book and cover design by Lucy Lesiak
Library of Congress Catalog Card Number 85-080904
ISBN 0-912500-20-4

CONTENTS

Foreword

Preface

Chapter 1
Profile of a Fussy Baby *1*

Characteristics of High Need Babies • Supersensitive • Intense
• Demanding • Can't Be Put Down • Unpredictable • Nurses All
the Time • The Outcome

Chapter 2
Why Babies Fuss *7*

How a Baby's Temperament Is Formed • Nature vs. Nurture
• Goodness of Fit • The Stimulus Barrier • Missing the Womb
• Need Level Concept • Importance of a Responsive Caregiver •
Mother as Organizer • How the Baby's Temperament Affects the
Parents • Testing Temperament • Improving Intelligence

Chapter 3
Right from the Start: Improving Your Baby's
Temperament 27

Peaceful Womb Environment • The Early Weeks • Parents' Law
of Supply and Demand • Attachment Parenting • Building Up
Your Sensitivity • What's in It for You and Your Child

Chapter 4
Crying Guide for New Mothers 43

Why Babies Cry • Crying—the Perfect Signal • Interpreting Your
Baby's Cries • How Much Do Babies Cry? • How a Cry Affects
Parents • Survival Tips • Mellowing Your Baby's Cries • Your
Sensitivity • Should Babies Cry It Out? • Crying and Child
Abuse

Chapter 5
Parenting the Colicky Baby 71

Profile of a Colicky Baby • Why Colic? • The Gassy Baby • The
Tense Mother/Tense Baby Syndrome • Milk Allergies • Food
Intolerance • Smoking • Evening Colic • When Will It Stop?
• Communicating with Your Doctor • Calming the Colicky Baby
• Colic Dance • Massage • Pacifiers • Medication • Survival
Tips

Chapter 6
Soothing the Fussy Baby 97

Moving in Harmony • Baby Carriers • Swings • Freeway
Therapy • Getting in Touch • Soothing Sounds

Chapter 7
Feeding the Fussy Baby 109

Breast or Bottle? • Breastfeeding Advantages • Substances in
Breast Milk That Cause Fussiness • Breastfeeding Difficulties
• Formula Feeding • Feeding Tips • Minimizing Air Swallowing
• Burping • Starting Solids • Weaning

Chapter 8
Fathering the Fussy Baby   127

*Father Feelings • Sexual Feelings • Helping at Home • The Care
and Feeding of New Mothers • Gentling Tips for Fathers*

Chapter 9
Nighttime Parenting of the High Need Child   139

*Why High Need Babies Sleep Differently • Sleep Survival Tips
• Nursing Down • Sharing Sleep • Bedtime Rituals*

Chapter 10
*How to Avoid Burnout in the Mothering
Profession*   145

*Causes of Burnout • Babies Aren't to Blame • Early Warning
Signs • Lowering Your Risk • How Fathers Can Help • Priorities*

Chapter 11
The Shutdown Syndrome   161

Effects of Crying It Out • Babies Need Attention

Chapter 12
Disciplining the High Need Child   171

*Difficulties with Discipline • An Approach to Discipline •
Attitude and Atmosphere • Realistic Expectations • Spanking*

Chapter 13
The Pay-Off   179

*The Outcome • Benefits of Attachment Parenting • Giving
Children • Sensitivity • Feeling Right • Trust • Benefits for
Parents*

Chapter 14
Jonathan: a Case History   191

Index 203

FOREWORD

I've spent many hours rocking, walking, dancing, and singing to a baby who just couldn't get comfortable or fall asleep. The fussiest of my babies was my sixth. By then I was comfortable with babies and had learned how to be an excellent baby soother. I thought I knew exactly how to calm and cuddle any baby. It was quite a shock when this baby arched her back and screamed even though I had nursed her, checked her diaper and other clothing to see if anything was hurting her, nursed her again, wrapped, then unwrapped her, and tried to feed her yet again. Nothing seemed to help. She just continued to scream while I danced and walked with her, took her outside, and then came back in again. It was a frustrating time of life for us both. She was healthy, the doctor assured me again and again, so I couldn't understand what was the matter. Why was she so fussy?

Dr. Bill Sears has written this book to help parents through trying times like these. He explains that a baby's cry is one of the loudest of all human sounds and that it activates a strong response in everyone within earshot. It is a sound that I, as well as most parents, hurried to quiet. But when our attempts to comfort a baby don't work, we become frustrated, angry, and miserable.

Dr. Sears suggests many ways to soothe a baby that you may not have thought of, including using "back to the womb" activities. The many new methods he outlines will help you to help your baby enjoy a more contented start in life.

Dr. Sears details ways for parents to interact with fussy babies. By describing them as high need babies, he helps us to understand them. He urges parents to have a positive attitude and to form a strong attachment to their fussy baby. The rewards will come. As he says, "Babies who grow up in a nurturing environment with strong mother-infant attachment show enhanced intellectual and motor development."

Physicians learn a great deal during their years of schooling. However, they learn even more about human beings through their own life experiences. Dr. Sears is a pediatrician and father of five. This, plus his close association with the parents of his patients, has given him the knowledge and background needed to write this book. He profiles the fussy baby and explains why babies fuss. He also discusses fathering the fussy high need baby, nighttime parenting, and parents' sexual feelings, their relationship with each other, and how this affects them and the rest of the family.

The chapter on burnout and how to avoid it includes a stress test which lists nineteen points to consider and evaluate. These red flags that signal imminent burnout can help parents avoid or at least better understand what may be contributing to their frustration as they parent their high need child.

High need babies often become high need toddlers. Dr. Sears's approach to discipline and the development of trust and self-esteem can help parents through these trying times as well. Wrapping it all up is a wonderful descriptive case history of Jonathan. You will enjoy reading this story as you see yourself and your child through new eyes.

Parents are often asked if their baby is "good." Most people equate the "easy" baby with the "good" baby. But good means different things to different people. Sometimes being good means being wakeful and learning every minute, growing in every direction at once. Maybe your high need child is on the way to being a genius or a leader in life, and you're helping now with your love, patience, and understanding.

Betty Wagner
Executive Director
Founding Mother
La Leche League International

PREFACE

A fussy baby can bring out the best and the worst in a parent. This book is designed to bring out the best.

During my fifteen years in pediatric practice and my experience as a father of five children, I have become increasingly aware of a group of special babies whom I call high need babies—babies who are otherwise known as fussy, difficult, or demanding babies. Early on I realized that fussy babies are misunderstood. Mothers would ask, "How long should I let my baby cry? Is it all right to pick him up every time he cries?" or "Is it all right to carry the baby all the time? Will it spoil him?" I was confused by these questions. The standard baby care advice suggested that parents "let the baby cry it out." But I was uncomfortable with this. It seemed unfair to both mother and baby. It was then I realized that because of their intense love for their babies, mothers are particularly vulnerable to advice about crying. But the advice was confusing them.

Five years ago I began to study the problem of why babies fuss. I began with the belief that babies do what they do because they are designed that way. There must be reasons for their behavior, and there must be advice to give the mother of a fussy baby that is right for her and her baby. I set out to find both the reasons and the right comforting advice.

In this book I will share with you what I have learned from my personal counselling of several hundred parents of fussy babies. Throughout this book you will find practical tips on calming the fussy baby as well as personal testimonies from parents who have been there and survived.

The main points that I wish to present to parents in this book are:

Why babies fuss and what to do about it.
Why it is important to recognize your baby's temperament early.
How the baby's temperament develops the parents' temperament.
How the child's personality development is affected for better or for worse by your style of parenting.

I hope that reading *The Fussy Baby* will enable parents to know their high need child better and to help their child feel right. I hope it will also help both parents and children to enjoy each other more. These special babies require special parenting. High need babies get used to a higher standard of living—and loving.

ACKNOWLEDGEMENTS

My heart goes out to the hundreds of parents who have shared their stories and contributed to this book. A special thanks to my family: to Martha, my wife, who by her untiring giving to our own high need children has taught me to respect the unerring insight of mother's intuition; and to our five children who by their unique individual temperaments have made us richer parents. A note of appreciation goes to the hundreds of high need babies whom I have personally attended and from whom I have learned much.

CHAPTER 1

Profile of a Fussy Baby

"Uncontentable, that's what you are," sang a tired mother to her fussy baby as they danced their daily 6:00 p.m. crying and comforting ritual. This mother was able to vent her feelings through song and a bit of tired humor that got her and the baby through fussy times of the day.

Later, this same mother asked me, "Why is my baby like this? Other mothers seem to have easier babies. Why do I have such difficulty handling my fussy baby? Am I doing something wrong?" Her questions are shared by thousands of new mothers who feel overwhelmed by the incessant demands of fussy babies, but who are driven by uncompromising love to continue comforting and mothering their babies in need.

In the first few days or weeks after birth, parents begin to pick up on clues as to the temperament of their baby. Some parents are blessed with so-called easy babies. Others are blessed with babies who are not so easy and who receive a variety of labels: exhausting baby, colicky baby, demanding baby, and fussy baby. The term "fussy baby" is a bit unfair. It implies that one or both members of the mother-baby unit are failing; the baby's demands are unreasonable or the mother is unfeeling or inept. Something must be wrong with the baby and/or with the parents. Instead of "fussy baby," I prefer to call this special type of baby the **high need baby**. This is not only a kinder term, but it more accurately describes why these babies act the way they do and what level of parenting they need.

Characteristics of High Need Babies

High need babies share certain personality traits. Every high need baby may not show all of these behaviors all the time. In my experience, around twenty-five percent of all babies have many of these traits at some point during early infancy. Here are the ways parents have described their high need babies to me.

"Supersensitive"

High need babies are keenly aware of their environment. Changes cause them to startle easily during the day and make it difficult for them to settle at night. "Easily bothered" is how one mother described her sensitive baby. These children have short fuses and are easily set off by any disturbances which threaten the security of their environment. This sensitivity often carries over into their reactions to unfamiliar caregivers, resulting in a high degree of anxiety about strangers. While parents may find this supersensitivity initially exhausting, it may be transformed from a liability to an asset later on, leading the child to be more aware of and curious about his environment.

"Intense"

High need babies put a lot of energy into their behavior. They cry loudly, laugh with gusto, and are quick to protest if their "meals" are not served instantly. They seem to feel things more deeply and react more forcefully. "He's in high gear all the time," observed a tired father.

High need babies protest intensely when their environment is not to their liking. But they also seem more capable of forming strong attachment bonds with their caregivers. A baby who strongly protests a separation from his parents is doing so because he is strongly attached to the parents. The intensity of the protests is proportional to the intensity of the attachment. A strong attachment bond with parents is one of the best preventive medicines against long-term fussy behavior.

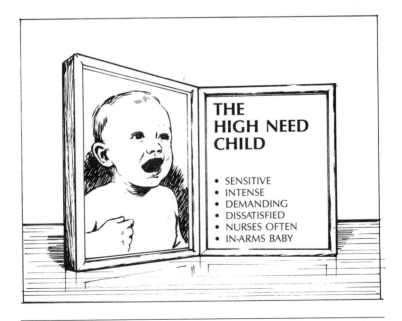

High need babies share certain personality traits.

"Demanding"

Mothers of high need babies often feel, "I just can't get to him fast enough." The baby conveys a real sense of urgency in his signals. "Red alerts" dominate his crying vocabulary. He has no respect for delayed gratification and does not readily accept alternatives if offered anything other than what he specifically cried for. If given a rattle when he is expecting to be nursed, his cries will intensify in protest at having been misread. Being demanding, however, is a positive and necessary character trait in high need babies.

"I Just Can't Put Him Down"

High need babies crave physical contact. New parents often unrealistically expect that babies will lie quietly in their cribs or sit passively gazing at interested onlookers and attentively playing with dangling mobiles. This is certainly not the play profile of the high need baby (or of most other babies). These babies are not known for their self-soothing abilities. Mothers tell me, "He can't relax by himself." Mother's lap is his chair, her arms and chest his crib, her breasts are his pacifier. Inanimate mother substitutes are often forcefully rejected by these babies.

"He's Always on the Go"

"There is no such thing as a still shot," said one photographer-father of a high need baby. "His motor seems stuck in fast idle," exclaimed another father. Constant motor activity goes along with the intense and supersensitive personality traits.

"Draining"

Parents inevitably confess, "He wears me out." A high need baby uses up all of mother's and father's energy.

"Uncuddly"

While most babies melt and mold easily into the arms and over the shoulders of their caregivers, the high need baby will often arch his back and stiffen his arms and legs, protesting any attempt to get him to conform to a comfortable nursing position. The term **hypertonic** describes this muscular tightness. "I can feel the 'wirey' in him," one mother related. The combination of supersensitive and hypertonic traits accounts for some babies' withdrawing from close physical contact. They resist being hemmed in and are more comfortable being held at a distance or facing away from you. They are often the babies who hate being swaddled as newborns.

"Unsatisfied and Unpredictable"
High need babies are inconsistently appeased. What works one day often fails the next. As one exhausted mother exclaimed, "Just when I think I have the game won, the baby ups the ante."

"He Wants to Nurse All the Time"
The term "feeding schedule" is not in the high need baby's vocabulary. These babies need prolonged periods of non-nutritive sucking for comfort and are slow to wean.

"Awakens Frequently"
These superaware babies do not settle easily. They awaken frequently and seldom reward mothers with much needed naps. "Why do high need babies need more of everything but sleep?" lamented a tired mother.

The Outcome

Early in infancy, most of the ways of describing the character traits of high need babies seem to be predominantly negative. This is a natural part of the history of parenting these special babies. I have observed that as the months progress, those parents who practice attachment parenting gradually begin to see their baby in a different light and use more positive descriptions such as challenging, interesting, and bright. Those same qualities which at first seemed to be such an exhausting liability have a good chance of turning out to be an asset for the child and the family later on *if* the baby's cues have been picked up on and appropriately responded to in the early months. The intense baby may become the creative child; the sensitive infant, the compassionate child. The little "taker" may later become a big giver.

Don't be too quick to predict what kind of person your child will become. Some difficult babies show a complete turnabout in personality later in childhood. But in general, the needs of these babies do not lessen; they only change.

What's in It for You?

One of the main themes of this book is that the temperament of the baby affects the temperament of the parents. In the following chapters, I shall discuss how a high need baby can bring out the best in responsive parents.

CHAPTER 2

Why Babies Fuss

"Why does my baby fuss and refuse to be put down?" asked a mother whose arms were giving out from constantly carrying her high need baby. One of the most frustrating feelings for parents is not knowing why their baby is fussing. In this chapter I want to give parents insight into why babies fuss and how baby and parents can influence each other's temperaments.

I use the term temperament to mean how a baby behaves, how he acts, the intent within him that makes him act the way he does. With time the child's reactions to the environment and the environment's influence upon the child develop this inner temperament into personality—the outward expression of the child's inner temperament.

How a Baby's Temperament Is Formed

Nature vs. Nurture

For decades, psychologists have debated the nature versus nurture question: whether it's primarily heredity or environment that determines the child's temperament. Today most scientists agree that a child's temperament is not a blank slate onto which caregivers can write a set of rules which will cause the child to act any way they wish. Neither is a child's temperament permanently cast in cement. Temperament certainly is changeable and able to be modified by the caregiving environment. Over the past thirty years, researchers in child development have become increasingly aware of how the quality and quantity of mothering and fathering can affect the child's temperament (White 1978; Sroufe and Waters 1982). One of the main purposes of this book is to illustrate how the caregiving environment can positively or negatively affect the temperament and eventual personality of the high need child.

Goodness of Fit

The goodness of fit principle describes one of the most powerful influences on a child's temperament. The principle states that how a baby or child fits into his caregiving environment will affect the development of his personality positively or negatively.

An infant comes wired with a temperament that is primarily genetically determined and perhaps is somewhat influenced by the environment of the womb. While in the womb, the unborn baby fits perfectly into his environment. Perhaps there will never be another environment in which the baby fits so harmoniously—a free-floating environment where the temperature is constant and nutritional needs are automatically and predictably met. This is an environment of total fulfillment, generally free of any stress (although the mother's emotional state may have some effect on the infant's temperament). In short, the womb environment is physically and emotionally very well organized.

Birth suddenly disrupts this organization. During the months following birth the baby tries to regain his sense of organization. Birth and adaptation to postnatal life bring out the temperament of a baby since for the first time he must do something to have his needs met. He is forced to act, to "behave." If hungry, he cries. He must make an effort to get the things he needs from his caregiving environment. If his needs are simple and he can get what he wants easily, he is labeled an easy baby; if he does not adapt readily to what is expected of him, he is labeled a difficult baby. He doesn't fit. Fussy babies are poor fitters, who don't resign themselves easily to the level of care they are being given. They need more.

The Stimulus Barrier

Why do fussy babies have a problem with this goodness of fit? First, fussy babies have an immature stimulus barrier. Babies are endowed with the ability to selectively block out and adapt to disturbing stimuli. For example, some babies will block out disturbing noises by falling asleep. These babies are very adaptable. Some babies have a stimulus barrier that is very permeable; they are unable to block out disturbing stimuli. These are the babies who receive sensitive and fussy labels. They are sensitive because they cannot adapt to disturbing stimuli, and they fuss in order to alert others to their need for help. These babies appeal to their caregivers to act as a stimulus barrier and help them fit into their environment better.

Missing the Womb

Another reason why babies fuss is what I call the "missing the womb" feeling. Being able to feel content is largely determined by the ability to adjust to change. A contented person feels his world is right for him and he is right for the world; in other words, he fits. The world of the unborn baby is a smooth continuum of experience in which he is lulled constantly by the sounds and movements of his mother and his needs are met consistently and automatically. Birth and the early weeks of adjustment may cause fussy tendencies to surface. The baby's expectation that life will continue as before is shattered, and the baby does not feel right. The newborn is unable to adapt to his new environment on his own, but he nevertheless has an intense desire to be comfortable. This conflict between wanting comfort and not being able to achieve it results in inner stress as well as outward behavior that is termed fussy. This baby is saying, "I expect to feel good but I don't, and I don't know what to do about it." When he fusses he is asking his caregivers to help him learn what makes him feel right and to give those things to him consistently until he can help himself feel right.

High Need Level

The need level concept explains another reason why babies fuss. Some babies come endowed with a high level of need. Their mothers say that "He never seems satisfied." In addition to high needs, these babies also come wired with the power to extract the necessary comforting measures from their caregiving environment. This is how these babies merit the demanding label. I want parents to view the demanding quality as a positive character trait that has survival benefits for the baby. If a baby were endowed with high needs yet lacked the ability to communicate these needs, his survival would be threatened and his emerging self-esteem would be in jeopardy. I feel that high need babies are inherently programmed to be demanding babies. This trait is especially noticeable in their crying behavior.

The most common example of demanding behavior in a high need baby is the baby who "cries whenever I put him down." Before birth this baby had a sense of oneness with the mother. After birth the mother knows that baby is now a separate person, but the baby does not feel separate. Baby still needs a sense of oneness with mother, birth having changed only the manner in which this oneness is expressed. This baby will protest or fuss if his attachment to mother is disrupted. He needs to continue the attachment a bit longer, and fortunately he has the ability to demand this. If this baby's needs are heard and filled, he fits; he is in harmony with his environment. He feels right. When a baby feels right, his temperament becomes more organized, and he becomes a "better" baby.

Throughout this book my central hypothesis is that high need babies fuss and have demanding temperaments because they *need* to be that way. Being fussy and demanding has survival benefits for these babies. If they didn't fuss, their needs might not be met.

What happens if a baby's needs remain unfilled because his demands have gone unheard? A need which is not filled never completely goes away but results in inner stress which sooner or later manifests itself as undesirable behavior, for example, anger, aggression, withdrawal, or rejection. This baby does not feel right and therefore, does not act right. A baby who does not act right is less of a joy to parent, and baby and parents drift farther and farther apart. The parent becomes less adept at giving, and the baby becomes less motivated to signal his needs. The entire parent-child relationship operates at a lower level.

The need level concept implies that your baby fusses primarily because of his own temperament and not because of your mothering abilities. Babies fuss because they have to in order to fit. However, the responsiveness of the caregiving environment does play a part in determining whether or not the baby's demanding temperament is channeled into desirable or undesirable personality traits.

Consider the goodness of fit and need level concepts from the baby's viewpoint. A high need baby who is trying desperately to fit into his environment may take one of two paths:

1. He can fuss and fuss until he receives the level of care he needs.
2. He can give up and resign himself to a lower standard of living. This means he will not develop his temperament to its maximum potential and instead may develop what I call disorders of shutdown: withdrawal, apathy, and developmental delay.

The Importance of a Responsive Caregiver

An important part of the goodness of fit is the response of the caregiving environment to the baby's needs. A high need baby with a demanding temperament needs a responsive caregiver in order to feel in harmony with his world and to develop his personality.

It is vital to the well-being of the high need baby that his world revolves around a central attachment figure, a secure home base of operations. This role naturally falls on the mother. A strong mother-infant attachment leads to the development of a trusting relationship. Because non-adaptability and disorganized behavior are the trademarks of a high need baby, the mother's role is even more important, since these babies need extra assistance to fit into their environment. It takes two conditions for this mother-infant bond to develop:

> The mother is available and increases her nurturing response proportionate to the needs of the baby.

> The baby shows attachment-promoting behaviors. Attachment-promoting behaviors include smiling, sucking, cooing, clinging, gazing, and some form of crying upon departure—in other words, the behaviors which make an infant irresistible.

A sensitive, responsive mother and a baby with good attachment-promoting behaviors are a good match, and a strong bond develops. When the baby does not show many attachment-promoting behaviors or the mother is unable to read and respond to the cues of the baby, the bond may not develop.

Attachment means that mother and baby are in harmony; they develop a oneness with each other and become a mother-baby unit. Baby gives a cue, and mother, because she is open to the baby's cues, responds. Baby enjoys the response and is then motivated to give more cues because he has learned that he will get a predictable and rewarding response. The result is that the mother and baby grow accustomed to each other. They enjoy each other. As one mother put it, "I'm absolutely addicted to her." Once mother and baby get addicted to each other, the mother's responses become more spontaneous and her parenting flows naturally.

Mothers with a strong attachment to their high need babies sometimes say that the baby "seems glued to me." They also use the term "unglued" to describe the feeling their babies have when they do not feel the goodness of fit with their environment. Nancy, a mother who had worked long and hard to develop a strong attachment bond with her high need baby, told me, "When the baby becomes unglued and seems to be falling apart, I now feel I can pick up the pieces and glue him back together. It has been a long tough struggle, but I am finally beginning to cash in on my investment." The strong attachment between mother and high need baby may be summed up in one word, sensitivity—mother and baby become more sensitive to each other.

Mother as Organizer

The mother plays a vital role in organizing her baby's behavior. This is easier to understand if you think of a baby's gestation period as lasting a full eighteen months—nine months inside the womb and at least nine more months outside. During the first nine months, mother's primary role is to nourish the baby and contribute to his physical development. The womb environment regulates baby's sensory and other systems automatically. But birth temporarily disrupts this organization. However, the more quickly a baby gets outside help with organizing these systems, the more easily he adapts to the puzzle of life outside the womb. After birth, the mother continues to nourish the baby, but her role expands into many more areas of the baby's development:

1. Nutritional: Mother provides nourishment with her milk.

2. Tactile: Mother provides physical contact.

3. Visual: Mother has a familiar face.

4. Auditory: Baby grew accustomed to mother's voice and sounds prenatally.

5. Thermal: Mother's body heat helps to stabilize the fluctuating body temperature of a tiny baby.

6. Vestibular: Carrying and rocking help the baby develop his own sense of balance.

7. Olfactory: A baby knows mother's familiar odor.

8. Sleep/wake patterns: By sharing sleep with their babies, mothers help them organize their sleeping habits into a predictable day and night pattern.

The baby's attachment to the mother has an organizing influence on his behavior. By anticipating and filling his needs, mother helps him adapt to a world where those needs are not automatically met. Without this attachment, the baby remains disorganized, and this results in fussy behavior.

Fussing is a withdrawal symptom, a result of the loss of the regulatory effects of attachment to the mother. This indicates that tiny babies should not be left alone to train them to become self-soothers, as some parenting advisors would suggest. Tiny babies should not be expected to function as separate individuals as soon as possible. Experimental evidence supports this. When newborn animals are separated from the regulatory influence of the mother, they show "increased behavioral arousal" (Hofer 1978), in other words, fussy behavior. Babies who are nursed to sleep are less likely to become habitual thumbsuckers than are babies who are left to soothe themselves to sleep (Ozturk and Ozturk 1977). Infants show more calm behavior when they're in touch with mother than when left alone (Brackbill 1971). Sleep disturbances are more common in babies who are separated from their parents at night (Sears 1985). Infants separated from their mothers show more unusual "self-rocking" behaviors (Hofer 1978). In my opinion, training babies to become self-soothers before they are ready and capable is as ridiculous as expecting a premature baby to be a self-provider of his own medical care.

How the Temperament of the Infant Affects the Temperament of the Parent

A mother of a high need baby once confided to me, "Our fussy baby absolutely brings out the best and the worst in me." This is certainly true. Just as babies come wired with different temperaments, mothers also have varying response levels. For some mothers, a nurturing response is automatic and is proportionate to the need level of their babies. For others, responses are not so automatic, and their nurturing abilities need to grow and mature. Understanding that a child's temperament affects the mother's nurturing ability is absolutely vital to the successful parenting of the high need baby. The baby's behavioral traits can affect the temperament and responsiveness of the parent in many ways.

Easy Baby/Responsive Mother

The so-called easy baby is a cuddly baby with good attachment-promoting skills whose needs are predictable and who just melts into the arms of anyone who holds him—the type of baby that everybody likes to be around. Because mothers tend to feel that the "goodness" of their babies reflects their effectiveness as mothers, the easy baby's mother

feels that she is doing something right and is delighted with the whole situation. A mother who is struggling along with a more difficult baby tends to feel that she must be doing something wrong.

Easy Baby/Less Responsive Mother

Because the easy baby is not very demanding, even a less responsive mother may need to expend relatively little effort in developing creative comforting skills. But this is not always so rosy. Because the easy baby seems so easily satisfied, the mother may tend to divert her energies into other more challenging relationships and activities such as a more difficult child in the family or an outside job. She may feel that the baby "doesn't seem to need me that much." This situation accounts for the **delayed fusser**, a baby who starts

---

"She Seemed Like Such an Easy Baby"

"Karen was such an easy baby. She never cried much. I could put her down for the night at 7:00 p.m., and she would sleep till morning. She seemed content with babysitters, which freed me up to do other things. But around four months, she started crying every time I put her down. She started awaking several times at night to nurse, and I finally had to sleep with her. She won't settle for any babysitter. Now I really feel tied down."

Karen is what I call a delayed fusser. She was a high need baby in an easy baby disguise who finally got up enough nerve to demand what she needed. Crying and night-waking are normal attachment-promoting behaviors which help the baby develop and mature the mother. This baby was simply not going to settle for a lower standard of living.

---

out easy and then around six months (or whenever mother's energies are diverted) makes a complete turnabout in personality. He becomes a fussy baby and suddenly unleashes a burst of attachment-promoting skills with which he demands a higher level of response from his caregiving environment.

High Need Baby/Responsive Mother

The next situation is the combination of a high need baby who has good attachment-promoting behaviors with a responsive mother. In this situation, parents cannot bear to ignore the incessant demands of the high need baby. His presence is always noticed. His cries demand an instant response, and once he has found his way into a comfortable spot in his parent's arms he refuses to be put down. Although this baby has high demands, the parents are rewarded by the feeling that their comforting measures are at least getting through to the baby. The occasional satisfied response from the baby gives them the feeling that it is all worthwhile. This type of demanding baby brings out the giving part of a mother's temperament. A high need baby with good attachment-promoting skills matures the mother's nurturing response—as long as she remains open and responsive and answers his needs without restraint. The mother must allow her intuitive nurturing to flow from her heart, uninhibited by the cultural norms of the neighborhood and unrestricted by conflicting advice from others. Even when the mother is confused because the baby's needs are difficult to identify, she experiments with alternate responses until she finds one that satisfies the infant. She becomes the baby's central attachment figure and develops the specific comforting skills that nurture her baby. Because the baby continually receives the nurturing response he anticipates, the baby refines his attachment-promoting skills. This in turn makes it easier to identify his needs and to comfort him. The entire parent-child relationship evolves into one of mutual sensitivity. The sensitive mother-infant pair enjoy each other more.

"She Was So Uncuddly"

"Rebekah was born into a family where mother, father, and two-year-old brother were all thrilled with her arrival. Having successfully nursed my son, I eagerly anticipated those same close moments with my daughter. But from the moment she was born, Rebekah showed little desire for cuddling. She would pull away from me after nursing and wriggle uncomfortably until I put her in her crib. She did not smile and avoided eye contact until she was nearly a year old. In spite of normal motor development, she indicated little interest in her surroundings. I shared my anguish and frustration with my pediatrician, but because he could find nothing organically wrong, he had nothing to contribute. I felt that somehow I had deprived this innocent child of something which was vitally needed—and yet I had no idea of what it could be. I really wanted to know her and to be close to her, yet there seemed to be an impenetrable wall between us.

"Shortly after Rebekah's first birthday, I became convinced that this behavior cycle needed to be broken. Very, very slowly we have seen some opening up in Rebekah. She has begun to share some of her feelings. With children her own age, she is becoming friendly and displays real leadership qualities. She still doesn't like to get too close, but on the whole, she seems to be better able to relate to her world and the people in it. She seems to need so much and yet is unable to receive."

The uncuddly baby is the most difficult high need baby to parent. These babies break the rules for promoting attachment. They do not smile, do not cry when they are put down, nor do they take any pleasure in nursing. As a result, mother must initiate attachment behavior and work hard to maintain it even though the baby is giving neither cues nor appreciation for what he receives. This baby does not automatically bring out the best in the mother. Instead, he requires the highest level of maternal giving in order for the mother to break through.

The High Need Baby with
Poor Attachment-Promoting Skills

These babies are often known as "non-cuddlers" or "slow to warm up." This baby withdraws and arches his back when picked up to be held and fed. He does not melt and mold to the contours of the parent's body when draped over lap, breast, or shoulder, and shows little or no appreciation for the mother's efforts to get through to him. Although in my experience most high need babies do tell their caregiving environment what they need loudly and clearly, there are babies who do not demand the level of nurturing that they need. Because parents, especially mothers, are generally geared to respond to a baby's signals, uncuddly babies do not bring out the best in mothers and may bring out the worst. In fact, studies have shown that mother-infant attachment is often less intense with non-cuddlers (Campbell 1979).

In order for a mother's nurturing responses to grow and mature, she must receive some appreciative feedback from the baby. (Babies and children are not noted for pouring out their gratitude to parents.) If the mother does not receive this feedback, she may be tempted to seek out alternative sources of fulfillment, and there is a danger that the mother and baby will drift farther and farther apart. In this situation **interaction counseling** really pays off. Mothers of non-cuddly babies who feel a bit shaky about their nurturing response ("I'm just not getting through") may do well to seek some counseling from professionals trained in mother-baby interaction. These are sensitive, experienced caregivers who can teach the mother how to pick up and respond to the more subtle cues of the non-cuddly baby. Mothers of uncuddly babies should beware of feeling that the baby "doesn't need me." This can deteriorate into feeling that "the baby doesn't like me." Uncuddly babies are often high need babies in easy baby disguise. They need the best responses the parent can give in order for the best in themselves to develop.

The High Need Baby and the Restrained Caregiver

A high need baby and a restrained caregiver are at risk for
not developing each other. In this situation the baby may
have good attachment-promoting behaviors, but the mother
tries to make a science out of child rearing. Instead of letting herself go and following the nurturing instincts of her
heart, she succumbs to the advice of well-meaning friends,
relatives, and advisors: "Let baby cry it out; you're making
him too dependent"; "You'll be sorry. You're picking him up
so often, you're spoiling him"; or "He's manipulating you."
Mothers of high need babies, beware of advice that suggests
you restrain yourself from responding to your baby. If you
are getting lots of this kind of advice, you are running around
with the wrong crowd of advisors. This advice will tear down
a mother-baby relationship because it confuses a new mother.
Mothers of high need babies are particularly vulnerable to
any advice that others promise will work. Beware especially
of quick and easy solutions that suggest adhering to rigidly
scheduled feedings, bedtimes, and periods of crying—for example "Let the baby cry forty-five minutes the first night, thirty
minutes the second night, and he'll sleep through by the end
of the week." This seldom works for any baby, but it is especially disastrous for the high need baby.

Rigid schedules don't even make scientific sense. Humans
are a continuous contact species; mothers and babies stay
close to one another. In some animal species, the mother
can leave her young for extended periods of time to gather
food. The mother's milk in these species has a high fat content which allows the baby animals to survive with widely
spaced feedings. Human milk, on the other hand, is relatively
dilute; it has a low fat and protein content which makes frequent, seemingly continuous feeding necessary. The mother
is programmed for immediate nurturing responses. When
she hears her baby's cries, the blood flow to her breasts increases, triggering the maternal urge to pick up and nurse
the baby. A mother who falls prey to the advice to restrain
her responses to her baby is going against her intuition and
her biology. Following the dictates of outside advisors which

run contrary to her heart is the first step toward making a mother insensitive to her baby. Insensitivity is the first step towards mother-infant detachment. However, an unrestrained response to a baby's cries brings out the mother's nurturing qualities and increases the attachment.

What about the effect of restrained responses on the baby? A baby whose signals are not responded to may take one of two directions. He may increase his attachment-promoting signals, become more demanding, and cry until someone finally picks him up. Babies who take this approach may expend so much energy demanding the attention they need that little energy is left over, and they slow down developmentally. Studies have shown that infants are developmentally advanced in societies where attachment parenting and immediate nurturing responses are the rule rather than the exception (Geber 1958). The other direction an infant may take when his signals are not responded to is to give up. Without a response, he is no longer motivated to communicate

---

Getting Over Anger

"Steven, our two-year-old, and I just weren't getting along. After a lot of soul-searching, I discovered that my anger was hurting our relationship. I was angry with Steven for not being the baby I had expected and for wearing me out and not being as easy to handle as other babies. As soon as I recognized this anger and dealt with it, we both enjoyed each other more."

In this situation, mother became angry because the baby she wanted was not the baby she got. Her anger toward her baby kept her from seeing her baby as an individual, a high need baby who needed a high level of mothering. When she realized that her anger was keeping her from relating to her child, she began to see him for the unique person he was and stopped comparing him to other babies.

---

his needs, so he shuts down his signals and withdraws into himself, attempting to survive emotionally on a variety of ineffectual self-soothing habits. The baby attaches to objects rather than persons. In this situation both parties of the mother-baby pair lose. Neither has been able to profit from the skill of the other. The mother's nurturing responses have not been matured by the baby, and the disorganized nature of the baby's behavior has not been organized by the mother. The end result is one of the most difficult relationships in parenting—mutual insensitivity.

Testing Your Baby's Temperament

Over the past ten years a variety of scales has been developed to evaluate the temperament and personality of infants (Brazelton 1973; Carey 1970; Thomas et al 1968). These scales rate nine behaviors that define temperament in infants: activity, rhythmicity, adaptability, approach, sensory threshold, intensity, mood, distractibility, and persistence. While these temperament tests certainly do help new parents evaluate the personality of their babies, I want to offer a word of encouragement to those parents whose babies may be rated as "difficult." A difficult rating is not always a liability. For example, being "generally fussy on waking up and going to sleep" would be a temperamental characteristic that would merit the baby points as a difficult baby. Suppose the baby fussed because he didn't want to go to bed *alone* but was happy when he was allowed to fall asleep in his parents' arms and awaken in their bed; that's not an unreasonable demand. Another example: The baby who is able to soothe himself when upset gets a point for being easy while a baby who fusses until someone comes to comfort him is rated difficult.

I suspect that these parameters of infant temperament do not assess the baby at all. Instead they measure how closely the baby conforms to cultural expectations of what babies ought to be like. This is different from how babies really are. Parents tend to equate easy babies with better babies, although the authors of these temperament tests caution against this. A baby who fusses when put to sleep alone or fusses if no one picks him up has the strength of character to assert his personality and tell his caregivers what he needs. This baby is learning to be attached to persons rather than things. It would be more accurate to designate the "difficult" baby as an "assertive" baby or an "attached" baby. These are more positive terms and more accurately reflect the character of the baby. The term "difficult" makes a judgment which reflects the expectations of the culture rather than the baby's temperament.

Improving Your Baby's Intelligence

Nurturing responses to a baby's temperament can enhance intelligence. I believe that each child is endowed with a maximum intelligence potential which is primarily genetically determined. The child also comes wired with a set of behavioral traits we call temperament. These traits are specifically designed to activate the child's environment to meet his needs. They elicit responses from caregivers which encourage the child's intelligence to grow through interaction with the environment. In the first few years, parents are the child's primary environment. If the cues of the child are responded to, the child becomes more adept at interaction because he can count on consistent feedback. For example, a child with a high intelligence potential may also come wired with the temperament traits that merit him the label of demanding baby. He demands to be held all the time, slept with, suckled; in other words, he demands a high level of attachment and interaction with his environment. Since interacting with his environment is one of the ways the baby can reach his intelligence potential, being a demanding baby is beneficial to the child with a high intelligence potential.

Although a child's intelligence potential is primarily genetically determined, the child's self-esteem is not genetically programmed, and here's where the caregiver response really pays off. As a pediatrician with a personal interest in fussy babies, I have long suspected that babies do what they do and act the way they do because they are designed that way. Perhaps babies with a high intelligence potential are designed to be demanding, especially in a culture that advocates restrained responses to babies. The baby with an assertive temperament (the high need baby) who also has a nurturing and responsive caregiver has the best chance to achieve his maximum potential. (The caregiver also has a good chance to develop his or her maximum potential as a parent.) This child learns to **trust**; he **fits** into his environment. He also learns to trust himself; in other words, he develops self-esteem. He gradually fusses less as his other communication skills develop. The child feels better about himself and therefore is able to interact more effectively with his environment. His intelligence keeps right on developing. Early on the baby fusses a lot because he needs a lot. As he gets older, his needs do not lessen; they only change. The child then learns to fuss less and communicate his needs in other ways.

What happens to the intelligence potential in a child whose cues are misread and whose assertive behavior is squelched—the baby who is left to cry it out? Because the child's intelligence and temperament complement each other, his intelligence may not grow if his temperament is not de-

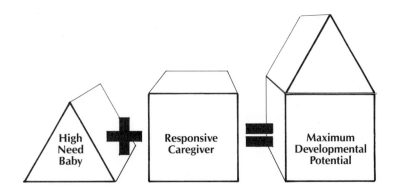

A responsive caregiver will enable a high need child to develop his full potential.

veloped. This is like a carpenter who has high aspirations to construct a great building. If someone keeps taking away his tools, either he'll never finish the building (that is, reach his maximum potential) or he will accomplish the feat at a much slower rate and with a great deal of stress and frustration. There are many studies to support the correlation between intellectual development and the caregiving environment (White 1978; Sroufe and Waters 1982; Geber 1958). Babies who grow up in a nurturing environment with strong mother-infant attachment behaviors show enhanced intellectual and motor development.

Stress and Intelligence
Nobel prize winner Hans Selye, in his book *The Stress of Life*, proposes that stress can enhance intellectual development. How a person reacts to a stressful situation and resolves that stress can have a positive or negative effect on intelligence. Fussy babies seem to exude a lot of inner stress, but they are often not endowed with the ability to handle their own stress. This is why it is even more important for the intellectual growth of a fussy baby that he receive a nurturing response to stress. Resolving this stress may enhance the infant's intellectual growth; unresolved stress may hinder it.

In this chapter I have presented an explanation of why babies fuss and how a baby's intelligence potential and temperament traits and the caregiver's responses all work together for the development of baby and parents. Subsequent chapters will explore practical ways to apply these ideas to parenting the high need baby and child in order to bring out the best in parents and baby.

References
Brackbill, Y. 1971. Effects of continuous stimulation on arousal levels in infants. *Child Dev* 42:17.

Brazelton, T. B. 1973. Neonatal behavioral assessment scale. In *Clinics in Developmental Medicine* No. 50. Philadelphia: Lippincott.

Campbell, S. B. 1979. Mother-infant interaction as a function of maternal ratings of temperament. *Child Psychiatr Hum Dev* 10:67.

Carey, W. B. 1970. A simplified method for measuring infant temperament. *J Pediatr* 77:188.

Geber, M. 1958. The psycho-motor development of African children in the first year and the influences of maternal behavior. *J Soc Psychol* 47:185.

Hofer, M. A. 1978. Hidden regulatory processes in early social relationships. In *Perspectives in Ethology*, P. P. G. Bateson and P. H. Klopfer, eds. New York: Plenum.

Lozoff, B. and Brittenham, G. 1979. Infant care: cache or carry? *J Pediatr* 95:478.

Ozturk, M. and Ozturk, O. M. 1977. Thumbsucking and falling asleep. *Brit J Med Psychol* 50:95.

Sears, W. 1985. *Nighttime Parenting*. Franklin Park, Ill.: La Leche League International.

Selye, H. 1978. *The Stress of Life*. 2d ed. New York: McGraw Hill.

Sroufe, L. A. and Waters, E. 1982. Issues of temperament and attachment. *Am J Orthopsychiatr* 52:743.

Thomas, A., Chess, S. and Birch, H. G. 1968. *Temperament and Behavior Disorders in Children*. New York: New York University Press.

White, B. 1978. *The First Three Years of Life*. Englewood Cliffs, N.J.: Prentice-Hall.

CHAPTER 3

Right from the Start: Improving Your Baby's Temperament

Certain characteristics of temperament may be necessary for the child to reach his fullest potential. These positive aspects of a baby's temperament can be refined, developed, and channeled into behavior which benefits the baby and the family. Two important stages in which parents can have a dramatic and often lasting effect on the baby's temperament are the last months of pregnancy and the first two weeks after birth.

The Importance of a Peaceful Womb Environment

Fetal awareness is a new and exciting field of research. The unborn baby is acutely aware of the joys and stresses of his environment, and his temperament can be affected for better or for worse by what he feels and hears during life in the womb (Liley 1972; Verney 1981). This section is for parents who are expecting a baby and can begin now to lower their risks of having a fussy baby as well as for parents who have already had a fussy baby and would like to decrease the chances of the next baby being fussy. Parents can begin using some behavior modification techniques during pregnancy. Most of the research on fetal awareness concerns the last four months of pregnancy, yet it is entirely possible that further research will discover that maternal behavior also affects the younger fetus.

You may be wondering how researchers can know so much about the fetus. Three noninvasive research tools have been used to study fetal emotions. The electroencephalogram (EEG) records changes in a baby's brain waves in response to changes in environmental stimuli. Ultrasound uses sound waves from outside the mother's abdomen directed toward the fetus. The sound waves bounce back through a sensor onto a screen, producing an image of the baby. Changes in the sound waves reflect changes in the fetus's behavior. A sophisticated photographic instrument called fiberoptics allows researchers to actually see how the baby is reacting to outside stimuli.

The basic assumption underlying fetal research is that you can tell how an infant feels by the way he acts. This may not always be a correct assumption. There is not a perfect correlation between the mother's emotional state during pregnancy and the temperament of the baby. A tense pregnant mother will not always produce a tense baby. A peaceful womb environment is just one of the many factors that affect the eventual temperament of your baby. What we are discussing in this section is just one of the many ways of lowering your risk of having a fussy baby.

How the Mother's Emotional State
Affects Her Unborn Baby

Mother and baby are part of the same hormonal network. Those same hormones which produce stress reactions in the mother (increased heart rate, increased blood pressure, flushing, sweating, headaches, etc.) also pass through the placenta to the baby. So when mother feels upset, baby is upset. Researchers theorize that if an unborn baby is continually exposed to stress hormones from the mother and is continually producing his own stress hormones in response to an anxious environment, he has a higher risk of developing an overcharged nervous system. As parents and others have said about fussy newborns, "It seems like he came wired that way." The following suggestions are aimed at creating a pleasant communication network between mother and unborn child.

Think the right thoughts. Research has shown that a mother's attitude toward her unborn baby may affect the baby's attitude toward the mother later on. An old obstetric axiom states that if a mother rejects a fetus, that baby may later reject the mother. While certainly there is no clear-cut cause and effect explanation for this (nor is it true in all cases), research has shown that mothers experiencing unwanted pregnancies have a greater likelihood of having fussy babies, and they themselves have a lower tolerance for fussiness. This is certainly not a joyful combination.

Sing the right songs. An expectant mother told me, "When my baby kicks and seems upset, I play music." Researchers in fetal awareness claim that babies, children, and even adults can recall songs that their parents sang to them in utero. Pregnant symphony musicians feel that music becomes a part of their babies before birth; music played by the mother during pregnancy was more easily learned by the child later on. Experienced mothers and fathers of fussy babies have related to me that the same lullabies and songs that they sang when their unborn baby was upset are the sounds that calm their babies after birth. These calming sounds have been imprinted on the mind of the unborn baby, and he has learned to expect and respond to them during postnatal upsets. One of Pat Boone's daughters, Lori, shared with me how she, now herself a mother, still is calmed by the songs her daddy sang to her while in the womb.

Agitated unborn babies are calmed best by classical music (for example, Vivaldi, Mozart, flute, and classical guitar), religious hymns, and folk songs. Fetuses have been shown to react violently to rock music. Dr. Thomas Verny, author of *The Secret Life of the Unborn Child* (1981), told of a mother who suffered a damaged rib at a rock concert because of her unborn child's strenuous kicks. Perhaps the violent display of fetal emotions was triggered by the aggressive overtones of the rock music. Many mothers can tell when their fetus is upset and which of their own songs or other music has a calming effect. Unborn babies seem to have highly selective musical taste. (As the father of two teenagers, I have begun to suspect that a child's musical taste deteriorates as he gets older.)

The songs and sounds that soothe your baby in the womb will also calm him after birth.

I advise mothers to keep a diary of those musical pieces which have a calming effect on their unborn babies so they can call upon these tunes later during trying times. Research has shown that a four- or five-month-old fetus hears and moves his body in synchrony to the rhythm of his mother's voice and songs. Just as pleasant sounds may soothe the infant, unpleasant, dissonant, and angry sounds may upset the unborn baby. The fetus has been shown to become agitated during times of parental fighting and will even move his hands over his ears when exposed to disturbing music.

Fathers, take heart, there is something in this prenatal symphony for you: Studies have shown that when the father talked to his baby in utero, the baby was more responsive to daddy's voice after birth. In my own practice, I have encouraged the prenatal custom of laying on of hands. I encourage expectant couples to lay their hands on the uterus every night before going to bed, and talk, sing, and pray for the unborn child. Not only does this soothe the baby, but I believe the child inside also senses commitment to the marriage and to parenthood when those two people who are nurturing him join hands over him. I advise fathers to orchestrate this symphony, as this is a way of getting in touch and in tune with your baby before birth. Fathers who have enjoyed this custom throughout the final months of pregnancy have later confided to me, "Now I'm hooked. I can't get to sleep at night until I first lay my hands on the head of our newborn and reaffirm my commitment." Mother's and father's voices and songs seem to be like an acoustic umbilical "chord" which is not severed at birth but continues for a long time thereafter.

Dance the right dance.   When your unborn baby seems agitated, experiment with various waltz-like dances until you find one that calms the baby. You may need to call upon this same dance step later on. One mother related to me that rhythmic swimming would settle her unborn baby.

Feel good feelings.   How a mother feels about herself during pregnancy may have a bearing on how the fetus feels
about himself. Researchers in fetal awareness believe that
the fetus is most affected by chronic and unresolved stress
in the mother. The fetus is much less agitated and less likely
to be permanently affected by acute normal life stresses that
are quickly recognized and quickly dealt with. Studies have
also shown that a mother's attitude toward pregnancy can
become a self-fulfilling prophecy (Verney 1981). Mothers who
were fearful of childbirth and expected a "war story" were
more likely to have a traumatic birth; the infants of these
mothers were more likely to be fussy babies. Women who

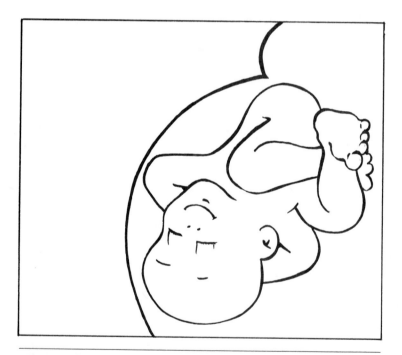

*Pleasant thoughts, soothing music, rhythmic motion, and a sense of
being loved contribute to a peaceful environment in the womb.*

were ambivalent about becoming a mother were more likely to have apathetic babies; it was as if the fetus picked up these mixed messages and came into the world confused and untrusting of his caregivers. Mothers who were downright rejecting of their fetus throughout their pregnancy were the most likely group to have emotionally disturbed infants. The mothers in this study who had pregnancies that were relatively trouble-free emotionally were the most likely to be in harmony with their babies after birth. In these fetal outcome studies, the single most important contributing factor to a mother's emotional well-being during pregnancy was the total commitment of a loving and caring husband. Fathers do indeed play a vital role in nourishing the temperament of their unborn children.

The womb environment establishes a child's expectations of the world to come. If the womb has been a harmonic and loving environment, the child is likely to expect the same from the world he enters, possibly predisposing him toward a cuddly, trusting, calm temperament. If the womb has been hostile, the baby may enter his world distrustful and detached and may not easily fit into his environment. This newborn's parents may describe their baby by saying, "He came out fighting."

While this research on fetal awareness is still in its infancy, I believe it is accurate to say that life will be more difficult for an infant delivered from a difficult womb environment than for a child who had a peaceful womb experience.

The Early Weeks

How a mother and baby get started with each other may have a profound impact on achieving two important parenting goals: smoothing out the temperament of the baby and building up the sensitivity of the mother. In this section I will present a parenting style which will help you achieve these two goals.

Parenting Economics: the Law of Supply and Demand
Every baby comes wired with a unique level of need, based
upon his individual temperament and ability to adjust to his
caregiving environment. Every baby is also endowed with
an instinctual ability to give cues to his caregivers, telling them
what he needs. Babies with higher needs give stronger cues.
For example, a baby who needs to be held all the time cries
when his caregiver attempts to put him down. Babies have
no problem giving cues; but recognizing these cues is a central problem in parenting the high need baby.

Every parent also has a certain level of ability to inter-
pret the baby's cues, a sort of radar system that stays tuned
into the baby. This is often called mother's (or father's) intuition. When the need level of the baby and the giving level
of the parent match, the pair is in harmony. When the needs
of the baby baffle the intuition of the parents, the family is
out of harmony. Years of observing parents and babies have
led me to conclude that a law of parenting economics ex-
ists in each parent-child relationship—the law of supply and
demand. **Parents will be able to meet the needs of their
individual child, providing they adopt a parenting style that
allows their intuition to mature so they can become more
sensitive to their baby's cues.**

Occasionally a mother will share with me, "Sometimes
I don't feel like I have any intuition. I just don't know what
my baby needs." One of the main purposes of this book is
to help parents build up their sensitivity to their baby. In my
past thirteen years in pediatric practice, I have observed how
some parents of high need babies build up their sensitivity
more than others. The most sensitive parents are usually the
ones who've adopted a style of parenting which I call **attachment parenting**. This style includes the following practices.

Prenatal preparation. Take a prepared childbirth class
which prepares you for the type of birth that *you* want: a
birth that will allow your baby the most natural passage possible, free of drugs, gadgets, interventions, imposed routines
and impossible positions, confinements, and separations that

agitate and disturb mother and baby. The transition from being inside the mother to being outside (but still *with*) the mother must be smooth and gentle. The prenatal period is also a good time to read as much as you can about the development of infant temperament (the references listed in this book are a good place to start) and get involved with some parent support groups. In my opinion, the support group that best prepares a mother to handle a fussy baby is La Leche League. This prenatal preparation period is also a time to strengthen your marriage bond and reaffirm your commitment to each other. A stable and fulfilled marriage is absolutely necessary for successful parenting of a fussy baby.

Dad's involvement in parenting begins during pregnancy.

A peaceful birthing experience.   There is a saying in pediatrics that an anxious birth may produce an anxious baby. Studies have shown that babies who are the product of a birth characterized by fear, pain, and mother-baby separation are more likely to become fussy babies. There is also a higher incidence of fussy and colicky babies among mothers who have been heavily medicated during childbirth (Meares 1982).

Bonding and rooming-in.   Unless medical complications make it impossible, arrange to keep your baby with you from birth on. This eases your baby's transition from the womb to the outside world. Having your baby room-in with you while you're in the hospital helps to smooth his temperament and builds up your sensitivity.

Off to a Bad Start

"I should have known something was wrong when I would hear the nurses calling, 'Michael, Michael' every night in the nursery. On the third or fourth night, though, I was not hearing his name being called. In fact, I was proud of myself because I had nursed my 'good' baby to sleep. 'This is easy,' I thought. 'How nice of the hospital to establish a four-hour feeding pattern for me.'

"When we went home on the fifth day after my cesarean, Michael seemed to fit right into a four-hour cycle. That lasted until about 8:00 p.m. on the first evening. The infamous fussy baby hour had begun, and so had night after night and day after day of no sleep. I was insecure about being a mother. I did not grow up around babies and knew nothing about taking care of them. I didn't know what to expect. In spite of all the advice and warnings to the contrary, the thing I focused on was that my girlfriend's baby who was two months older than Michael had slept through the night ever since he was born.

"Needless to say, by the second day home I was angry

Off to a Bad Start *(continued)*

and frustrated, and by day three I was wondering why I had ever wanted a baby. The incessant nursing really drove me out of my mind. Michael would nurse for the longest time but would be satisfied for such a short time. I wanted to do the best thing for my baby, but I dreamed of bottles, particularly at night.

"Everyone told me new mothers should sleep when the baby sleeps, but I could not fall asleep during the day. In fact, I couldn't even relax. I expected to hear Michael cry at any given second.

"No other mother in my entire family had ever breastfed successfully. They told me, 'He must be hungry. Babies just don't cry all the time.' Besides this subtly jealous or defeatist attitude about breastfeeding, I knew that Michael's constant need for attention was driving them crazy. This was not a baby that ate and went to sleep. This baby ate, dozed, ate, and cried, cried, cried. He never seemed to be satisfied.

"Finding out from Dr. Sears that this was simply (!) the high need baby syndrome was somewhat of a relief, but when I got home and sat down in my rocker to nurse Michael, I began to cry. I felt that I could not cope with a baby like Michael. That sense of despair has only gradually diminished.

"At about two-and-a-half months Michael began responding and doing all the things that make having a baby fun. At about eight months he started sleeping fairly consistently. Despite the inconvenience and horrible feelings I went through, I'm glad I persisted because I have one of the happiest and most secure babies that I know."

This baby learned to fuss because a rigid four-hour schedule was imposed on him in the hospital nursery. It took this mother eight months of "catch-up" parenting to mellow her baby. The mother's advisors were too quick to jump on breastfeeding as the cause of the fussiness. This mother needed more positive support and less negative advice.

Breastfeed your baby.   Unrestricted breastfeeding helps a mother to become more sensitive to her baby's cues. It also helps baby develop better communication skills because mother responds to his fussiness with a predictable nurturing response—nursing. Allowing the baby to wean himself helps develop his internal feeling of rightness.

Respond promptly to your baby's cries.   Promptly responding to baby's cries develops your sensitivity to his unique language. It also teaches the fussy baby to cry more effectively.

Nighttime parenting.   Fussy babies tend to awaken easily because they carry their sensitive temperaments into their sleep patterns (Sears 1985). Welcoming your baby into your bed (the concept of sharing sleep) helps baby organize his sleep patterns and awaken less.

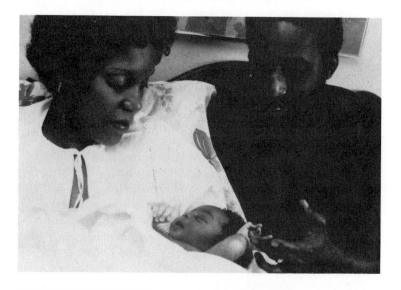

Keeping baby with you in the hospital helps you to know each other right from the start.

Travel as a unit.   Keep your baby with you. Travel as a father-mother-child unit. This strengthens your commitment to parenting and enhances your sensitivity to your baby and to each other.

Father involvement.   Mothers who have coped well with a high need baby often tell me, "I could not have survived without the support of my husband." High need babies—and their mothers—need active involvement from fathers.

Attachment Parenting: What's in It for You?

Builds Up Your Sensitivity

The attachment style of parenting begins with a spirit of **openness**, being open to the cues of your child and being open to the intuition of your heart. Openness to your child is the first step in becoming a sensitive parent. The attachment style of parenting helps mother and baby be in harmony with each other. Starting off the parent-child relationship in harmony is the best preventive medicine for the fussy baby.

Increases Your Mothering Hormones

The attachment style of parenting builds a "hormoneous" as well as a harmonious relationship. Being in touch with the baby, unrestricted breastfeeding, and sleeping with the baby raise mother's prolactin levels. This hormone, which regulates the production of breast milk, may also be the chemical basis for mother's intuition. I like to think of prolactin as a perseverance hormone that gives mothers an extra boost during trying times. You may be thinking that the attachment style of parenting is all giving, giving, giving. But bear in mind that when mothers are open and giving to their babies, the babies give something back by stimulating mothers' prolactin. This mutual giving occurs when you let the mother-baby relationship operate the way it was designed to.

May Lessen Baby's Fussiness

Many babies will start out as easy babies, but around two weeks of age (after what I call the "grace period") they make a complete turnaround and become difficult. Mothers will often relate, "He was such an easy baby the first couple of weeks, but now he's a different person." I feel that some of this delayed fussing could be prevented by giving the babies greater harmony in their environment. These babies do not feel the goodness of fit and as time goes by, they begin to protest to tell their caregivers that change is in order.

What's in It for Your Child?

He Feels Better

A baby who is the product of an attachment style of parenting feels right. A baby who feels right acts right. These babies don't have to begin fussing to get what they need or at least they don't have to fuss for long. They learn to fuss better. This internal feeling of rightness mellows the internal stress and disorganization that characterize many fussy babies.

He Grows Better

Besides behaving better, babies parented with the attachment style show advanced physical and intellectual development. Babies who have a strong mother-infant attachment use the mother as the prime energy source for meeting needs and comforting in times of stress. As a result, these babies don't spin their wheels. They waste less energy in ineffectual self-comforting measures and instead, use their energy for growth and development.

The Outcome

At this point parents may be wondering, "Does it make any difference what style of parenting the difficult or fussy baby receives? Can I really affect the way my infant turns out?"

The answer is a resounding yes! I do wish to caution parents not to take too much blame or credit for the way their infant turns out. There are infants who despite good parenting develop behavioral problems later on in childhood. But studies have shown that parenting styles do make a difference.

References

Liley, A. 1972. The fetus as a personality. *Aust NZ J Psychiatr* 6:99.

Meares, R. et al. 1982. Some origins of the 'difficult' child. *Brit J Med Psychol* 55:77.

Sears, W. 1985. *Nighttime Parenting*. Franklin Park, Ill.: La Leche League International.

Verney, T. 1981. *The Secret Life of the Unborn Child*. New York: Dell.

CHAPTER 4

Crying Guide for New Mothers

"If only my baby could talk, I would be able to know what she wants," exclaimed a new mother. "Your baby can talk," I responded. "You need to learn how to listen." This chapter is about interpreting your baby's crying. It will help you:

Understand why babies cry.
Improve your listening skills.
Increase your sensitivity.
Train your baby to cry better.
Lessen your baby's need to cry.
Prevent a crying baby from becoming a whiney child.

In preparation for writing this chapter I sent out several hundred questionnaires asking parents about commonly given advice. One of the questions was, "What advice do you get about responding when your baby wakes up crying or cries to be held all the time, or when he cries if you put him down?"

The most common advice parents received was:

> "Let him cry it out."
> "He's got to learn to be independent."
> "He's manipulating you."
> "Crying is good for his lungs."

Another part of my questionnaire asked parents how this advice made them feel. The most frequent responses were:

> "I can't do it."
> "It goes against my instinct."
> "It doesn't feel right to me."
> "I can't let her cry when I know I have the means to comfort her."

Ninety-five percent of mothers responded that the advice to let their babies cry didn't feel right to them. Since I have learned to place great value on mothers' gut feelings, I have concluded that ninety-five percent of mothers can't be wrong. This questionnaire also showed me that there is an incredible conflict between mothers' intuition and what other people are telling them.

Because of this widespread confusion about the meaning of an infant's cry and the proper way to respond to it, this chapter is the longest and most detailed in the entire book. It is important because your understanding of the communication value of your baby's cry carries over into many other aspects of your parenting. It upsets me as a pediatrician that babies' cries are so poorly understood. I feel like an attorney pleading the case for my little client who does not yet have the language skills to stand up before his caregivers and say, "Please hear me out."

Why Babies Cry

In the first few months of a baby's life, there is a real paradox: a baby's needs are the greatest at a time when his skills to communicate these needs are least effective; a baby cannot tell us in plain language what he needs. To fill this gap in time in which the baby is unable to communicate clearly, the baby has been given a language which we call a cry. Since communicating with language involves at least two people, a talker and a listener, if a baby doesn't cry both the baby and the parent are in trouble. Although a cry is not always the plain language that parents want, you can be sure that when a baby cries, he needs something. That's a good place to start.

> But what am I?
> An infant crying in the night,
> An infant crying for the light,
> And with no language but a cry.
> *Alfred Lord Tennyson*

There is probably no other sound that has been studied as extensively as the infant cry. What is it that makes the infant cry so disturbing? Scientists have long been fascinated by the way the sound of a tiny infant can compel all within earshot to come to attention. Charles Darwin was interested

in the cries and the facial expressions of infants in his book *The Expression of Emotions in Man and Animals.* When Thomas Edison invented the phonograph in the early 1900s recordings began to be used to study infant cries. The earliest reports of infant cry studies came in 1932 from William Gardener in *The Music of Nature,* a book in which he describes the cries and calls of infants by means of musical notes. He found that the tones of cries usually fall between middle C and the A above it on the piano. "Children," he wrote, "have no difficulty in expressing their wants, their pleasures, their pains by their cries, long before they know the use or meaning of a word." Scientists have found that the infant cry is one of the loudest of all human sounds, ranging from eighty to eighty-five decibels—equivalent to the noise of an unmuffled truck.

Crying: the Perfect Signal
How does the cry work? The infant first senses a need. The realization of this need reflexively triggers the sudden inspiration of air followed by a forceful expiration. The forcefully expelled air passes the vocal cords, and the vibrating cords produce a sound we call a cry.

This signalling system has several unique features. First, the cries of early infancy are of reflex origin; they are **automatic**. A tiny infant does not have to stop and think, "Now, what kind of cry will get my dinner served?" This initial reflex crying is later refined into more purposeful and deliberate crying as the infant's communication skills develop. Second, the signal is **easily generated**; the infant initiates crying with very little effort. Third, the cry is **disturbing** enough to alert the caregiver to attend to the baby and stop the cry, but not so disturbing as to provoke an avoidance response. Fourth, the cry **vanishes** when the need for it is past. All of these features make the infant cry a perfect signalling system.

A cry is not just a sound; it is a **signal**. Cries are triggered by needs, and babies will use different signals for different needs. The stronger the stimulus, the more forcefully the air is expelled, and the vocal cords vibrate more rapidly. This accounts for the difference in the quality of the sounds produced. Researchers call these unique sounds **cry prints**. These are similar to voice prints which are studied by experts and which are as unique to each individual as fingerprints.

How to Interpret Your Baby's Cries

Cries of Pain

Pain cries begin suddenly, reach a high pitch quickly, and then seem to stay at that high pitch for an eternity. The initial opening sound is shrill and shrieking. Toward the end of the first breath of the cry, the pitch tapers off as the baby begins to run out of breath. The inspiratory sound is harsh, almost croupy, as the infant quickly builds up a new supply of air power for the next yell. The initial shrill piercing sound of the pain cry goes right to the heart of anyone within earshot. Toward the end of the first breath, the caregiver's emotions are aroused also by how the baby looks. The mouth is wide open as if to say "ouch." The baby's furled tongue and open jaws quiver; his face grimaces. His fists are clenched, legs drawn up, and the baby's whole body is tense. The part of the pain cry that really gets to me is toward the end of the breath when baby's quivering lips begin to turn blue and just for a moment no sound is produced; finally, the baby takes his next breath. This "blue period" of the pain cry has a "red alert" signal value even though little sound may be produced during those frantic few seconds.

There is a total body language to pain cries. To be fully appreciated, the baby's cry needs to be seen as well as heard. In fact, studies have shown that even experienced mothers cannot always decode the meaning of their babies' cries if they cannot see the baby.

The baby's face reflects the intensity of the cry. In a cry of mild distress a baby's eyes are open, and only the area around the mouth is contorted. As the crying intensifies, the signs of distress travel up the baby's face: closed eyes, wrinkled eyebrows, and furrowed forehead. You should get used to watching your baby's facial features for reflections of his needs; this will help you become attached to your baby. An attached mother is unable to tolerate hearing her baby cry if she is close by and able to see the baby.

Cries of Hunger

Hunger cries begin less suddenly and build up more gradually. They are shorter and less shrieking and have a sustained high frequency and a rising and falling melody. The hunger cry contains frequent pauses, as if giving mother at least a few seconds to get her blouse up before the baby starts another round of more intense signals. Cries that signal basic needs tend to contain more pauses, as if the infant anticipates a reaction and is giving the caregiver time to respond. Before the cry starts, there are other telltale clues of hunger: restlessness, mouthing the fingers, nuzzling at the mother's breast, and a whole barrage of other warning signals that give the mother a chance to respond even before a cry is necessary. Reading the hungry baby's body language can often avert the need to cry. Hunger cries that are left unsatisfied can mushroom into all-out cries of anger.

Cries of Anger

Anger cries are sustained cries with a pronounced vibrato. They are pitched lower than pain or hunger cries. The body language that accompanies them is more intense. The hoarse sounds throughout cries of anger are caused by the turbulence of excess air being forced through the vocal cords. Sometimes there is a bubbly sound to the cry as the air vibrates the saliva in baby's throat. The lips are often a clue to the anger cry. The mouth is more closed and the lips tightly clenched, pursed and overlapping as compared to the open-mouthed cry of pain. This difference is more noticeable in older children than in tiny babies.

Cries during Illness

The cries of an infant who just isn't feeling well tend to be of lower pitch and intensity. They are weepy, whiney, and prolonged and stir up more of a sympathetic feeling than an immediate red-alert response. These cries contain more low-pitched "uh, uh" sounds than the more shrill pain cries.

"I Want Attention" Cries

Bored cries are whiney, low-pitched, murmuring sounds that get noticed but do not set off an internal alarm in the listener. Most parents easily decode baby's "pick me up and do something with me" cries.

Tired Cries

When a baby is crying because he's tired, the cries are longer in duration and have a noticeable vibrato and a wailing siren-like sound.

I advise new parents not to spend too much energy figuring out why their baby is crying. This energy is better spent responding to the cries. You can learn as you respond.

How Much Does the "Usual" Baby Cry?

Most studies of crying babies show that babies begin to cry more often around two weeks of age. The amount of crying peaks around six to eight weeks and then markedly subsides around the fourth to sixth month. Many studies state that infants cry "an average of two to three hours each day." I urge parents to beware of drawing any conclusions from these studies of crying. These studies, which are widely quoted, often conclude that it is normal for babies to cry two to three hours a day. I do not personally believe this. In my own practice and personal experience I would certainly not consider it normal for babies to cry two to three hours a day. The reason I caution parents about putting much faith in these studies is that I don't want parents to conclude that it is all right to let their baby cry two to three hours a day. The mothers in these studies were not given any counseling about what to do when their babies cried and were not specifically advised to use all possible mothering skills to keep their babies from crying. In cultures in which an immediate nurturing response is the normal response to an infant cry, the amount of daily crying is reported in terms of minutes, not hours.

How a Baby's Cry Affects the Parent

The infant cry is more than just a sound. It is a signal with value—an expressive signal with the intent of influencing the behavior of another. An infant cry has survival value; it helps the baby get the things he needs by **activating** or **releasing** the mother's emotions (Murray 1979). Using the terms release and activate implies that something is ready in the person on the receiving end of the cry, especially in the mother. Studies have shown that women in general respond to an infant's cries more intuitively and with less restraint than do men. The survival value depends upon the infant properly emitting the cry, and the listener correctly perceiving it. The infant's cry does something to the mother's body chemistry, and that's what makes it so special. When a mother hears or sees her baby cry, certain hormones are released, and there is an increase in blood flow to her breasts (Vuorenkoski 1969). This is accompanied by an urge to pick the baby up and nurse and comfort him. There is no other sound in the world that will trigger such intense emotions in the mother. Fathers are more likely to fall prey to the "let the baby cry" advice because they have no such biological response to a baby's cries.

A sensitive mother told me once how guilty she felt when her husband discovered their two-day-old baby crying in their bedroom. He carried the baby, still upset and crying,into the family room, and when the mother saw her squalling newborn, she was instantly overwhelmed with guilt. Up until then the baby had been kept near her, within hearing and seeing distance. This time she had not been available to recognize the pre-cry signals, and the baby's body language made it obvious that he had been crying for several minutes already. She recalls this vividly two years after the event took place.

Even little children have built-in responses to babies' cries. One day a mother brought her two-year-old daughter and her one-month-old baby into the office for an exam. When the baby began to cry, the two-year-old quickly ran to her mother, pulled on her skirt, and exclaimed, "Mommy, baby cry. Pick up." The mother then said, "She's always like that. I can't get to her baby sister fast enough." In our own family I love to see how our six-year-old daughter, Hayden, gives an immediate nurturing response to the cries of her two-year-old sister, Erin. We call this the "zoom" response. Whenever

---

"I Feel So Guilty"

"Shut up and leave me alone," screamed Janet at her four-month-old baby who had been crying incessantly. Later she reported, "I feel so guilty about yelling at him."

Janet's ambivalent feelings are shared by thousands of mothers of high need babies. A mother's love and concern for her high need baby make her particularly vulnerable to feelings which shatter her image of herself as a perfect mother. Even though she is not acting on her angry emotions, Janet feels guilty because perfect mothers aren't even allowed to feel angry at their babies. This belief is not true.

Mothers can get themselves in a real anger bind. They may feel angry towards their babies for being so difficult and not responding to comforting measures. They feel angry at themselves for not being able to comfort their fussy babies, and they get even angrier with themselves because they feel angry with their babies. Every mother I have ever counselled feels angry at her baby at some time. This anger stems from frustration at not being able to get through to the baby. It can also be the product of disappointment because the baby you got was not the happy, peaceful baby you expected. Janet's feelings of guilt are a normal reflection of her love and sensitivity toward her baby.

Erin wakes up from her nap with a cry, Hayden is off like a flash, breaking all speed records to go and comfort her little sister.

A cry also has a disturbing effect on the listener. The mother especially is likely to feel, "I can't stand to hear him cry any longer." A cry cries to be turned off. The ideal cry is disturbing enough to elicit attachment or comforting behaviors, but not so disturbing as to put off the listener. Cries are primarily attachment-promoting behaviors which draw mothers and babies closer; however, the incessant cries of a fussy baby may have a negative or alienating effect on the mother. The cries of a baby stimulate empathy in the parent; that is, the parent shares in the baby's emotionally painful state. Parents of a fussy baby may get tired of "feeling for that baby." The strong love between parent and child makes parents particularly vulnerable to the stress of these empathic feelings. If you have a fussy baby or feel that you have a fussy baby, realize that you start out at a higher risk of developing an unhealthy interpretation of your baby's cries. Studies have shown that mothers who perceive their infants as difficult early on and who are more restrained in their responses

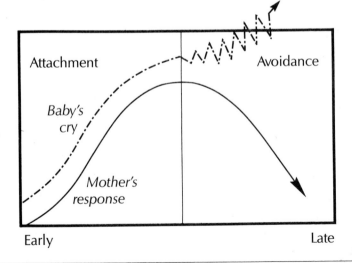

The Crying Hill: As the infant's cries become more disturbing, the mother's response goes "over the hill" from attachment to avoidance.

to the baby's cries are less likely to engage in reciprocal vocalization with their babies later on (Shaw 1977). In general, caregivers tend to misjudge the cries of fussy babies more often than those of easy babies. They are also more likely to call a difficult baby "spoiled."

Because of the fussy baby's nature, his cues are more intense. The increased intensity of these cries may initially promote more intense attachment behavior. However, these intense cries may also become increasingly disturbing, resulting in what I call the "over-the-hill" response. The person on the receiving end of the cries gets overloaded, and the cries begin to provoke an avoidance response. A certain amount of avoidance is normal and healthy; it preserves your sanity. But a pattern of increasing avoidance responses and decreasing attachment behaviors is an early warning sign of a disturbance in the mother-infant relationship. It may be a time to seek professional help from someone who has an empathic understanding of why babies cry and what mothers can do to comfort them.

Survival Tips

Since crying is a language between a talker (the baby) and a listener (usually the mother), survival tips can be directed at both members of the crying communication network. You can learn how to minimize the disturbing qualities of your baby's cries by training him to cry better. You can also build up your sensitivity to and tolerance of your baby's cries.

Mellowing Your Baby's Cries

A peaceful postpartum period. Many babies do not show fussy behavior until around two weeks of age when the more disturbing crying seems to begin. I call this the two-week grace period. I suspect that some babies are born with a potentially fussy temperament, but they give their caregivers a two-week opportunity to mellow their temperaments. If the babies don't receive the help they need, the fussing begins.

Most babies, however, show their true colors soon after birth. You can usually spot a high need baby even as a newborn. It's as if right after birth the baby looks up and says, "Hi, Mom and Dad. I'm an above-average baby, and I need above-average parenting. If you give it to me, we're going to get along fine. If you don't, we're going to have a bit of trouble down the line."

Mellowing the baby's cries should begin immediately after birth. Parents and baby should be able to spend some time together, getting to know one another. Rooming-in during the time mother and baby are in the hospital continues this bonding process. Studies have shown that both mother and baby profit from rooming-in together. Infants of rooming-in mothers cry less. Mothers who room-in exhibit more mature coping skills with their crying babies postpartum (Greenberg 1973). The infant distress syndrome (fussiness, colic, incessant crying) is more common in infants delivered in hospitals where babies are kept in central nurseries rather than with their mothers (Craven 1979).

A critical look at the practices of many hospitals reveals this scenario: The newborn infant lies in a plastic box. He awakens hungry and cries along with twenty other hungry babies in plastic boxes who have all managed to awaken each other. A caregiver who has no biological attachment to the baby—no inner programming tuned to that baby—hears the early attachment-promoting cries and responds, as soon as time permits. The crying, hungry baby is taken to the mother (if he hasn't given up by this time) with little urgency. The mother, meanwhile, has missed the opening scene in this biological drama because she was not present in the nursery when her baby first cried. But she is expected to give a nurturing response to a baby who by this time has either given up crying or is "over the hill" on the crying curve and is now greeting the mother with more intense, disturbing cries. The mother, who has the biological attachment to the baby, hears only the cries that are more likely to elicit agitated concern or even an avoidance response. So even though she has a comforting breast to offer the baby, she is so tied up in knots that her milk won't let down, and the baby cries even harder. The mother feels like a failure as the "experts" in the nursery take over with a bottle of formula. This leads to more separation, more missed cues, more breaks in the attachment between mother and baby, and they leave the hospital together as strangers.

Contrast the nursery baby with the rooming-in baby. He awakens in his mother's room, maybe in her arms. His pre-cry signals are promptly attended to and he is put to the breast even before he needs to cry. If the baby does cry, it is the initial attachment-promoting cry, which when given a prompt nurturing response, never has a chance to develop into a disturbing cry. The attachment-promoting cries elicit a hormonal response in the mother, her milk lets down, and the mother and infant are in biological harmony. Nursery babies cry harder, but rooming-in babies cry better.

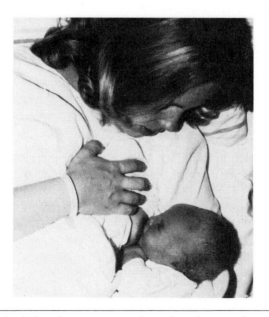

*The baby who rooms-in with mother does not have
to cry hard to have his needs taken care of.*

Unrestricted feeding schedules.   Rigid feeding routines lead to excessive and unnecessary crying (Bernal 1979). Feeding babies whenever they show signs of hunger prevents hunger cries from turning into more disturbing cries. Babies nurse for comfort as well as for nourishment; they should not have to wait until a set time.

Respond promptly to your baby's cries.   Babies who receive an immediate nurturing response to their cries eventually cry less frequently and with less intensity. When they do cry, their cries are less disturbing.

Carry your baby.   Get used to "wearing" your baby. Babies who are carried a lot cry less. A recent study showed that three extra hours of carrying a day reduced the amount babies cried by forty-five percent (*Pediatric News* 1984).

Building Up Your Sensitivity

Develop a healthy attitude towards crying.   Besides training babies to cry better, parents can also learn to listen better—to increase their sensitivity. This means fine-tuning your receiver to decode the signal of the baby's cry as well as building up your tolerance so you can persevere during those trying times when even the best parenting doesn't seem to be able to comfort and calm the baby. Beginning with the first meeting with your newborn, think of your baby's cry as a signal to be valued, not a habit to be broken. This starts your crying communication network off on the right "note." Your baby's cries are a language to be listened to, fine-tuned, and responded to.

Act, don't think.   Be spontaneous in reacting to your baby's cries. When your baby cries, the first little blip that comes in on your radar system is your intuition. Follow your feelings and act immediately and without restraint. Don't stop and think, "Why is he crying? Is he trying to manipulate me? Am I being taken advantage of? Am I spoiling him?" If you feel the urge to analyze your response to your baby's cries, wait until afterwards. Restraining yourself from responding to your baby's cries until you have figured it all out changes this beautiful mother-baby communication network from an intuitive art into the science of "cryology," which simply doesn't work. A baby's cry is a baby's own unique language. No two babies cry the same, nor are any two mother-baby communication units wired alike. To develop this sensitivity you must be open to your baby's cries and not restrain your responses. Take a risk. Your first impulse will probably be the right one.

Some mothers will confess, "But I just don't feel like I have any intuition. I really don't know why my baby is crying." It isn't as important to know why your baby is crying as it is to simply respond to your baby. I strongly believe that there is within each mother a built-in radar system (intuition) that will eventually be fine-tuned to her baby. The key to the fine-tuning is to create the conditions which allow this inner consciousness to develop. Being open to your baby's cries and responding to them immediately allows this intuition to develop. Restrained responses hinder the development of intuition. Some mothers take a little longer to develop this crying sensitivity, and some babies take a little longer to respond to a mother's comforting measures, but the two of you will get together as long as you let the communication flow as it is designed to do.

Building up your sensitivity chemistry. Breastfeeding mothers have high levels of a hormone called prolactin. This is often referred to as the mothering hormone. Prolactin is probably the chemical basis of mother's intuition and may be one reason mothers have a more intuitive nurturing response to cries than fathers. I have also referred to this hormone as the perseverance hormone. Building up your chemical sensitivity means building up your level of prolactin.

Sucking stimulates prolactin. It is the frequency of sucking, even more than the intensity, that has the greatest effect on prolactin levels. Thus unrestricted breastfeeding builds up your prolactin.

Spending more time with your baby also increases your prolactin levels. Touching, grooming, and just snuggling up close to your baby will increase your sensitivity to him. Looking at your baby, talking to him, having eye-to-eye contact are other ways of getting your prolactin going. Sleeping with your baby increases your prolactin. Science is beginning to prove what intuitive mothers have known all along—that something good happens to babies and mothers when they spend more time with each other.

Examine Your After-Cry Feeling

From time to time examine how you feel after you have responded to your baby's cries without restraint. I think that within each mother there is an internal sensor. She feels right when she responds correctly and feels wrong when she does not. An internal guilt light goes on when a mother does not respond appropriately. These internal sensors were built into mothers as added insurance that the young would be adequately mothered.

Picture yourself as having an internal computer with several response buttons. One is labeled, "Red alert: jump up and respond immediately." Another button is labeled, "Sit tight and hold off a bit." Still another button is for a response somewhere in between the first two. If your baby cries and you push the right response button, there is an inner feeling of rightness about your response. If your baby goes to "Red alert," but you press the "Sit tight and hold off a bit" button ("because my mother-in-law told me I'm spoiling him"), the result is an internal feeling of "not right." The guilt light goes on, and your inner computer says, "Not right. Something's wrong in the system."

A sensitive mother of a high need baby told me the following story: "My baby was wearing me down. So one night

when he woke up with his usual demanding cry at three a.m.,
I decided to let him cry it out. Boy, was he mad! I'll never
do that again. I felt so guilty. His crying was bad for both
of us." I responded, "You have developed a healthy guilt system. This means that you are well on your way to becoming
a sensitive mother." When it comes to responding to your
baby's cries, no one else can push the right button for you.
Your baby's crying circuitry is plugged into your computer
alone. It's not compatible with anyone else's computer.

The Ultimate in Sensitivity

A mother whose baby had been all but glued to her since
birth told me, "My baby seldom cries. She doesn't need to."
The ultimate in sensitivity to your baby is to be so tuned-in
to your baby's cues that he does not have to cry to get what
he needs. Admittedly very few mother-baby pairs reach this
level of harmony. But the attachment style of parenting that
I have suggested throughout this book gives parents a greater
likelihood of reaching this degree of sensitivity.

Mothers and fathers who practice attachment parenting
are tuned into their baby's stress indicators and will often
respond before the crying starts. The older the infant the
easier it is to read the signals. When our two-year-old daughter, Erin, looks up at me with raised arms, she is giving me
a "Daddy, pick me up" message. If I miss her opening cue
she may give me a second chance by whimpering a bit, and
if I still don't respond, this whimper develops into an all-out
cry. Since I have never had a particularly high tolerance for
babies' cries, we have found it easier in our home to create
a sensitive environment so that our babies seldom have to
cry to get what they need.

Let me prepare you for an objection that some people
may throw at you, based on behavioral psychology. Behav-
iorists tell you that if you pick your baby up every time he
gives the signal, you are reinforcing manipulative behavior
and "spoiling" the baby. As a self-appointed attorney in the
"Stamp Out Restrained Parenting Movement," let me offer

a defense. If you quickly respond to the *pre-cry* signals, you are reinforcing *these* signals. When you do not respond to the opening signals, you teach your baby that all-out crying is the best way to get quick results. This is much more likely to "spoil" the baby. By being sensitive to the pre-cry signals, you are reinforcing the development of other types of communication and body language (for example, squirming, nuzzling, vocalizing, and reaching). As your baby becomes more verbal and more capable of soothing himself, you will find that your response time can comfortably lengthen.

A New Look at Old Advice

Unwarranted fears of spoiling babies have characterized the parenting styles of the last thirty years and have given rise to a flurry of confusing advice concerning responses to babies' cries. I'd like to change the lyrics of the old song to "Look what they've done to my *cry*, Ma." Over the past several decades misguided child-care writers have increasingly attempted to tell parents how to control the normal sounds of babies. In my opinion, they have succeeded only in producing a fussier generation.

Should Baby Cry It Out?
Should babies be left to cry? No! When someone gives you the "cry it out" advice, ask what he or she means. You'll probably receive an answer something like this: "Well, he's only crying out of habit as a way to manipulate you." Then ask, "How do you know he's not crying because of a need?" As the dialogue goes on, your advisor should become increasingly aware of how unfair it is for someone to judge the language of a tiny baby without having all the facts, especially someone who has no biological attachment to that baby.

Why is the "cry it out" advice so common? Understanding the thinking behind this advice will help you understand how it became so widespread.

Rigid, restrained parenting.   The "let your baby cry" advice is a carry-over from the era of parenting that preached restraint. That was the period when there was an unwarranted fear of babies "manipulating" vulnerable parents. Parents were led to expect quick and easy methods for controlling their children. The "let the baby cry it out" advice fit in nicely with the rest of the program, which also included rigid schedules, formula-feeding, and doing everything by the book.

Parents were led to believe they could expect quick results from rigid methods of parenting. A good example is the classic dictum, "Let your baby cry for one hour the first night, forty-five minutes the second night, and by the end of the week he'll sleep through the night and there's the end of your problem." Parents, remember that difficult problems in child care do not have easy answers.

*A child who is left to cry it out is more likely
to be clingy, whiney, and "spoiled."*

Spoiling. "But you'll spoil the baby by picking him up every time he cries." This was another reason given to justify
the "let your baby cry it out" advice. Spoiling is one of those
unfortunate ideas that crept into child-care language and got
a firm hold in discipline concepts before anyone really ana-
lyzed what the word meant. The analogy does not work exactly the way the advocates of letting the baby cry might
think. For a basket of fruit to spoil, you have to leave it alone
on the shelf and let it rot. So it follows that children whose
cries are not promptly responded to are *more* likely to be
"spoiled." In fact, you can tell people who fear that prompt
responses to a baby's crying will turn him into a clingy, whiney
child that research has shown just the opposite. Studies at
Johns Hopkins University (Bell and Ainsworth 1972; 1977)
show that children whose mothers had responded promptly
to their cries as infants were less likely to use crying as a
mode of communication at one year of age. These children
were more likely to develop other social signals such as
gestures, facial expressions, and vocalizations to communicate with their parents.

Parents are led to believe that if they pick up their baby
every time he cries, he will not learn to settle himself and
will become more demanding as time goes on. This is not
true. A baby whose cries have been promptly responded
to early on learns to trust and to anticipate that a response
will be forthcoming. As this baby gets older, usually around
six months, that anticipation time gets longer, and both
mother and baby are content to wait longer before activating and responding to the crying signal. Time invested early
on gives you more time later.

Many studies have shot down the spoiling theory (Murray 1979; Shaw 1977). Babies whose cries are not promptly
responded to often learn to cry longer and with more disturbing cries. Studies have shown that mothers will often tend
to interact less with babies who have prolonged disturbing
cries. When these babies stopped crying as they got older,
the mothers still interacted less with these children. Why?
The mothers had become insensitive to the babies' cries, and

this insensitivity carried over into their later parent-child relationship. The advice to "let the baby cry" spoils the whole family.

Discipline. "You must discipline your baby" is another attempt at justifying the "let your baby cry" advice. This comes from the days when discipline was confused with control (as opposed to the sense in which I use the term discipline, motivating the child from within). Instead of developing a parenting style which is so tuned-in to the baby that he has no need to cry or at least learns to cry more effectively, parents stopped a baby's crying by not listening to it, thus squelching the signals. In my opinion a parent first has to listen to the baby in order to learn how to gain control of the whole situation. Unless the parents are open to the baby's signals, the baby cannot play a part in his own discipline. Throughout this book I have pointed out how this fear of openness has led parents wearily down a path of non-discipline; it keeps parents from laying the two vital cornerstones for effective discipline: knowing their child and helping their child feel right.

"Crying is good for babies." "It's good for his lungs" is another example of misguided information that contributes to a more restrained approach to babies' crying. Studies show absolutely no beneficial effect of crying, certainly not of prolonged crying. In one study, during unresponded-to crying episodes, babies' heart rates went up to worrisome levels (over 200 beats per minute), and the oxygen in the blood was diminished (Dinwiddie 1979). As soon as these crying infants were soothed, their cardiovascular systems rapidly returned to normal. Even the heart of a baby cries to be comforted. Crying is as good for the lungs as bleeding is for the veins. Babies who are left to cry it out by themselves can develop hoarseness that lasts for several days.

Another piece of erroneous medical folklore states that crying signifies a healthy baby. After birth a baby gets two extra points on his Apgar score for "crying lustily." As a former

---

"But I Did Everything Right"

"Thirteen months ago I gave birth to a baby boy. I had read a lot of books. I had been teaching childbirth classes and had prepared myself thoroughly. I had a healthy pregnancy with little stress, an excellent diet, and lots of exercise. I had an easy labor using the Bradley relaxation methods. We stayed at the clinic for two hours after the birth and then the three of us went home. I did everything right. Alex slept next to me and nursed all night. I 'wore' him in the baby carrier, responded to his cues, and nursed on demand. I expected to have a calm, serene transition to motherhood. I was extremely confident.

"Alex turned out to be a colicky baby, screaming every evening for three to five hours. He never napped and cried whenever I put him down. He didn't like the carrier, went on a nursing strike at two months, had three tantrums at four months, screamed when we went anywhere in the car, and wouldn't touch a bottle. My confidence turned to self-doubt and despair. My friends all took a much more rigid approach with their children, and they criticized me frequently, telling me I was raising a monster who was too dependent on me and was trying to control my life. That was hard to take. I was a very confused mother.

"I know I am past a lot of this now with Alex, but with my next baby I'm going to have the real confidence I lacked before. Also, I plan to have new friends. I am now seeking out other mothers who have chosen to meet their children's needs as I have. I know my friends meant well, but they didn't help me at all."

The important point of this letter is the statement "I did everything right." This mother did not cause her baby's fussiness. Even "right from the start" babies fuss. It's important to surround yourself with friends who share your mothering style. Otherwise you can become confused because your friends can erode your confidence.

---

director of a university hospital's newborn nursery, I have come to believe that the state of quiet alertness is more beneficial to the newborn than crying lustily. Crying is so "good" for toddlers that they often hold their breath and faint when a crying spell gets out of control. Besides being of no benefit to the lungs, recurrent unattended-to crying episodes may be detrimental to the baby's overall development. Some researchers claim that too much unattended-to crying delays the development of visual-motor skills, perhaps by diverting so much energy into self-soothing (Torda 1976a).

How the "Cry It Out" Advice Affects the Mother

Confuses mother's intuition.   Mothers find the "let your baby cry" advice confusing. It goes against a mother's own intuition. A baby is not designed to be left to cry, and the mother is not designed to let the baby cry. Mothers, your baby's cry and your responsive feeling is a unique mother-baby communication network designed for the survival of the young and the maturation of the parent. Ignore any advice that interferes with this communication network and doesn't feel right to you. Some new mothers are a bit shaky in trusting their own intuition over the advice of "experts." They may even feel guilty for not following the advice; love for their babies makes them vulnerable to any suggestions that they might not be doing the right thing for the baby. I believe that trusted advisors should not be confusing new mothers like this.

Desensitizes mothers.   Restraining her responses desensitizes the new mother to her baby. The "let the baby cry" advice encourages mothers not to listen to their baby or to their instincts. Some child care books in the past even contained the admonition, "Mothers, harden your hearts." If a mother continues to listen to someone else's advice instead of her own instincts and continues to ignore her baby's cues, she learns not to trust either herself or her baby. Lack of trust is the first step toward insensitivity, and insensitivity is what gets new mothers into trouble.

How Does the "Cry It Out" Advice Affect the Baby?

Not responding to a baby's cries undermines trust. The development of a trusting relationship with a primary caretaker is one of the prime determinants of an infant's personality. A child learns to trust as he is trusted. The more an infant trusts his own early crying cues, the more motivated he is to develop better communication skills.

The "cry it out" advice is often applied to nighttime situations. This can have damaging long term effects. Children remember thoughts and emotions which occur just before drifting off to sleep. One day on a radio talk show, I explained why parents should not leave babies alone to cry it out. The next day one of my patients brought her five-year-old boy, Timothy, into my office. The mother told me, "We heard you on the radio yesterday. When you told the story about how sad a child was whose parents were leaving him cry in his crib alone, Timothy said, 'The poor little boy. I remember when you and Dad left me to cry.'"

"Nobody Picked Me Up"

"I have always wondered how much of my mothering efforts my baby will remember when he is older. The following story has convinced me that my mothering does indeed have long-term effects.

"A twenty-two-year-old friend of mine recently tried to commit suicide. During intense psychoanalysis following her attempt, she revealed a flashback from when she was a tiny baby lying alone in her crib, crying helplessly. She broke down into tears, crying, 'I felt so alone, and nobody would pick me up'."

Memory researchers believe that we never completely forget anything; all events, especially traumatic ones, are permanently imprinted in our minds. I believe that high need babies, because of their supersensitivity may have particularly good memories.

Occasionally a parent will tell me, "But it works." This restraint advice may "work" with the easy, self-soothing baby (although there are good reasons for not allowing easy babies to cry it out). It seldom "works" for the high need baby. In my questioning of several hundred parents nearly all said they couldn't let their babies cry; the majority of those who tried it said it didn't work. Remember the mother who restrained herself from giving a nurturing response to her baby's cry? The baby kept right on crying and got angrier and angrier. The mother herself said, "I'll never do that again." Her guilt and the baby's anger revealed that something had gone amiss in the previously trusting mother-baby communication network. The non-responding (I think it's a non-responsible) approach is based upon the psychological principle of reinforcement and non-reinforcement. If a behavior is not reinforced or responded to, it goes away, a response that is coldly termed extinction. This is exactly what happens when the "let your baby cry it out" advice works; baby's mode of communication is extinguished and something inside the baby dies. I have great difficulty understanding this approach. By not giving in to your baby's cries, you teach your baby to give up, to despair. Both of you wind up losing.

I believe that there is a strong case against letting the baby "cry it out." I hope that my advice will help babies cry better and help parents listen better. When babies cry, someone should listen.

Crying and Child Abuse

One day when I was counseling parents of a high need baby, the mother inadvertently referred to her baby as a high risk baby. In a way, she was right. High need babies have a higher risk of being abused.

The ideal cry is powerful enough to elicit a sympathetic response from the caregiver, yet is not so disturbing as to trigger either an avoidance response or anger. Incessant disturbing crying can provoke child abuse. An analysis of cases of child abuse provoked by crying showed that the communication network had already broken down in these parent-child relationships (Ounsted 1974):

1. Parents who battered their babies were more likely to have practiced a style of parenting characterized by restrained responses.

2. These parents were more likely to label their babies as "difficult."

3. The battered babies generally had a more disturbing quality to their cries.

The communication network broke down because the babies' cries were not responded to promptly from early infancy. These babies learned to cry harder instead of to cry better. As a result the cries became more disturbing and released angry emotions rather than sympathy in a parent already at risk of being abusive.

Early counseling and coaching might have trained these parents to understand the signal value of their infants' cries. By teaching the potentially abusive parent to respond promptly and sympathetically to the baby's cries, the baby learns to cry more effectively, right from the start. The baby's cries will trigger empathic responses in the parent rather than releasing the parent's anger. The prevention of child abuse is just another example of the good that can happen when parents and babies learn to listen to each other.

References

Bell, S. M. and Ainsworth, M. D. 1972. Infant crying and maternal responsiveness. *Child Dev* 43:1171.

————. 1977. Infant crying and maternal responsiveness: a rejoiner to Gewintz and Boyd. *Child Dev* 48:1208.

Bernal, J. 1972. Crying during the first 10 days of life and maternal responses. *Dev Med Child Neurol* 14:362.

Brazelton, T. B. 1962. Crying in infancy. *Pediatrics* 4:579.

Craven, D. 1979. Why colic? *Med J Aust* 2:225.

Dinwiddie, R. et al. 1979. Cardiopulmonary changes in the crying neonate. *Pediatr Res* 13:900.

Greenberg, M. et al. 1973. First mothers rooming in with their new-born: its impact upon the mother. *Amer J Orthopsychiatr* 43:783.

Meares, R. et al. 1982. Some origins of the difficult child: the Brazel-ton scale and the mother's view of her newborn's character. *Brit J Med Psychol* 55:77.

Murray, A.D. 1979. Infant crying as an elicitor of parental behavior: an examination of two models. *Psychol Bull* 86:191.

Ounsted, C. et al. 1974. Aspects of bonding failure: the psychopathol-ogy and psychotherapeutic treatment of families of battered chil-dren. *Dev Med Child Neurol* 16:447.

Pediatric News. July 1984. Carrying infants can reduce their crying.

Shaw, C. 1977. A comparison of the patterns of mother-baby interac-tion for a group of crying, irritable babies and a group of more amenable babies. *Child Care Health Dev* 3:1-12.

Torda, C. 1976a. Effects of postnatal stress on visual and auditory evoked potential. *Perceptual Motor Skills* 43:315.

Torda, C. 1976b. Why babies cry. *J Am Med Women* 31:271.

Vuorenkoski, V. et al. 1969. The effect of cry stimulus on the tempera-ture of the lactating breast of primipara: a thermographic study. *Experientia* 25:1286.

CHAPTER 5

Parenting the Colicky Baby

If you are wondering whether or not you have a colicky baby, you probably don't have one. The colicky baby leaves no doubt in the minds of sympathetic caregivers that he is truly in agony. There is a large overlap between babies who are fussy and babies who are colicky. In this book I will refer to screaming babies as colicky if the cries have primarily physical causes and as fussy if the cries stem primarily from baby's temperament. I want to emphasize right at the outset that what you do about a baby's cries is more important than what you call them.

Profile of a Colicky Baby

Colic is not a disease; it is a syndrome. It has a number of symptoms. A colicky baby screams from intense physical discomfort. He draws his legs up onto a tense gas-filled abdomen and clenches his fists, seemingly angry at having this uncontrollable pain. The colicky baby communicates this pain to his parents who feel as helpless as he does at determining the cause of and alleviating the pain. The violent and agonizing quality of the colic cry drives parents to the edge. The cry of a colicky baby is paroxysmal, occurring in sudden and unexpected outbursts. Bewildered parents will often say, "He seemed perfectly happy and content just a minute ago. Now he's a wreck."

Frequent "ouch" signs are characteristic of colic's pain cries. The most disturbing feature of the colic cry is the body language that accompanies it: anger, tenseness, flailing of arms and legs, clenched fists, facial grimaces, and a hard tummy. The baby's arms are clenched tightly close to his chest and his knees are drawn up so tightly they nearly bump his bloated abdomen. Periodically during these attacks the infant may throw out his arms, stiffen his back, arch his neck, and dart out his legs, a move resembling a frantically executed back dive. Babies often fall into a deep sleep after the colicky episode is over.

The unrelenting nature of colic attacks is what usually gets to parents. Colicky spells may last a few minutes to a few hours, with occasional pauses of calm before the next storm breaks. By some perverse quirk of justice, colic seldom occurs in the morning when parents and infant are well rested; it usually occurs in late afternoon or early evening when parental reserves are lowest. In contrast to fussy high need babies who fuss all day, some colicky babies are relatively easy to handle when they're not having colicky periods. One mother told me, "He seems like two different babies, Dr. Jekyll and Mr. Hyde." On the positive side, colicky babies are the picture of good health. They tend to eat more and grow faster than non-colicky babies. The thriving appearance of the colicky baby often causes onlookers to remark, "My what a healthy looking baby. You're so lucky." Worn-out mothers respond, "You should have seen us a few hours ago."

Medical researchers have attempted to come up with a uniform definition of colic so that they can more accurately compare the results of studies of colic (Illingworth 1954; Wessel 1954). The definition includes the following components:

Occurs in otherwise healthy thriving infants.
Paroxysms of inconsolable crying without any identifiable physical causes.
Begins within first three weeks.
Lasts at least three hours a day, three days per week, and continues for at least three weeks.

The number of hours, days, and weeks are arbitrary figures. Colic symptoms vary widely from baby to baby and from day to day in the same baby.

Why Colic?

The most frustrating part of parenting the colicky type of high need baby is that seldom does anyone know the cause for a particular baby's colic attacks: not parents, not the pediatrician, not even the wise old grandmother. This has a significant effect on the parents' sympathy for a colicky baby. Physical causes of pain have a way of eliciting sympathy. It is much easier to comfort a person who is hurting when there is a readily identifiable medical cause for the hurt. While unknown causes also bring out a sympathetic response from parents, they do run the risk of creating reactions like "I'm being manipulated" or "I've been had." These feelings may add a bit of restraint to the caregiver's nurturing responses.

The term colic means an acute, sharp pain in the abdomen. Because this pain was originally thought to be caused by gas in the colon, it was labeled "colic." There are many popular myths and theories about the causes of colic. Many of them are only myths; they do not stand up to a critical look.

"Oh, He's Just Full of Gas!"

In the long and often fruitless search for the cause of colic, gas has often been implicated.

During colicky periods, the infant's tummy does seem more distended, and he passes a lot of flatus. Colicky babies often have many stools each day (probably because they eat so much). While the diapers usually contain large stools, mothers will often notice small amounts of diaper soiling from a little bit of stool that accompanies the forced expulsion of air.

During eating and digestion, the presence of food or air in the stomach stimulates the entire intestine to undergo a rhythmic squeezing and pumping. This moves the food and air from the stomach through the intestine, a process called peristalsis. Some researchers feel that intestinal peristalsis is immature and slower to develop in the colicky infant (Brennemann 1940). However, if intestinal immaturity were a cause of colic, it follows that colic would occur earlier in premature infants. This is not the case.

X-ray studies also cast some doubt on the theories that intestinal gas is the culprit in colic (Paradise 1966). Abdominal x-rays of non-colicky infants frequently reveal a lot of distention of the intestines with gas, but the infants do not seem to be uncomfortable. X-rays taken during and after colic crying spells showed no gas during the crying episode but a lot of gas afterwards. Air is gulped and swallowed during crying. Distention of the intestines by gas may be the *result* rather than the *cause* of colicky crying.

This is yet another reason why a prompt response to crying is important, especially in infants with a low pain threshold. Aborting the crying episode may lessen the amount of air the baby swallows, thus decreasing the amount of intestinal gas and shortening the duration of the colic cry. Those infants who are truly gassy babies should be trained to cry better. A prompt response is the first step in doing this.

Pain cries and anger cries are the most prone to air swallowing. These cries have a very long expiratory component, ending in a "blue period" of voiceless crying followed by a sudden forceful inspiration, as if the baby was trying to catch up on all the breath that was missed during the expiratory cry. This sudden gasping may cause more air to come in at one end than can be handled at the other. The air then accumulates in the intestines as gas, and colic results.

The Tense Mother/Tense Baby Syndrome

Colicky behavior in the infant is sometimes unjustly blamed on the mother. Some observers claim that the mother transfers her own anxiety to the baby, and the baby reacts accordingly. In most cases of colic this just isn't true. Colic occurs in babies of accepting, easygoing mothers as well as in babies whose mothers are more prone to be anxious. This is an important point because the behavior of the baby is often unjustly used as an index of the "goodness" of the mother. It is true that mothers vary widely in their coping abilities and that colic, like any stress that is not quickly dealt with, can be prolonged and reinforced by the tenseness of the mother. Some studies have shown absolutely no correlation between the personality of the mother and colicky behavior in the baby (Paradise 1966). Other studies have shown that mothers who score high on the anxiety portion of personality tests are more likely to have colicky babies (Carey 1968). Mothers who are tense, anxious, and depressed during their pregnancy are also more likely to have colicky babies. It is important to remember that most of the mothers in these studies who rated themselves as anxious did *not* turn out to have fussy babies; there is no absolute correlation between a mother's emotions and her having a colicky baby. Some studies also show that colic may be the result of a self-fulfilling prophecy. Mothers who expect to have trouble with their babies are more likely to have fussy babies. In my opinion, the emotional make-up of the mother has more influence on the handling of the colicky baby than it does on the causes of colic. A tense baby doesn't settle well in tense arms.

Milk Allergies and Colic

Infants whose colic is caused by food allergies are known as "allergic crampers." In the majority of colicky infants there is no relationship between the type of milk feedings and colic. The search for the "right formula" is generally fruitless. Most studies show no difference in colic incidence between breastfed and formula-fed babies; in my experience however, breastfeeding mothers often exhibit better coping skills.

A recent study has implicated allergy to cow's milk as a cause of colic (Lothe 1982). In a study of sixty severely colicky infants who were fed cow's milk formula, eighteen percent showed improvement when switched to soy formulas. Another fifty-three percent showed improvement when switched to a predigested formula. The authors concluded that "seventy-one percent of these infants became symptom-free after dietary therapy." However, any form of colic treatment is likely to have a placebo effect: just doing something produces an improvement in symptoms, even if the treatment is a placebo, something known to have no actual effect on the problem. This makes the design of colic studies very tricky. It is difficult to determine how much of the improvement in this particular study was the result of the formula change and how much was merely a placebo effect. Because infants who are allergic to cow's milk are also more likely to be allergic to soy formula and because some essential minerals, such as zinc, may not be absorbed from soy formulas, the American Academy of Pediatrics Committee on Nutrition recommends that soy formula not be used routinely in colicky infants (1983). You should consult your doctor before changing from one type of milk feeding to another.

Colicky reactions in breastfed babies may be the result of cow's milk drunk by the mother. Cow's milk allergens may enter the mother's milk and irritate her baby. This is still a controversial subject, but investigators have shown that eliminating cow's milk products from a breastfeeding mother's diet may lessen colic symptoms (Jakobsson and Lindberg 1983). Sixty-six mothers of breastfed infants with colic were put on a diet free from cow's milk. The colic disappeared in thirty-five infants; it reappeared on at least two challenges (giving cow's milk to the mother) in twenty-three of these infants.

However, another study (Evans 1981) raises doubts about the association between cow's milk and colic in breastfed infants. In this study of twenty breastfed infants with colic, the investigators found no relationship between the breast-feeding mother drinking cow's milk, the presence of cow's milk antigen in the breast milk, and the symptoms of colic. Although the final answer on the relationship between cow's milk and colic is not yet in, dietary manipulation in mother and baby is certainly worth a try, especially since colic can have such a devastating effect on the whole family. A note of caution: breastfeeding mothers should not change their diets without proper nutritional advice.

Other Food Intolerances and Colic in Breastfed Infants

Do gassy foods produce gassy babies? I've found a discrepancy between mothers' reports and nutritional science. Nutritionists believe that there is no scientific rationale for thinking that foods the mother eats get into her breast milk and produce gas in the baby. But occasionally a mother will tell me that she notices colicky symptoms in her baby within a few hours after eating certain foods. The foods most commonly reported as causing symptoms are:

Raw vegetables: broccoli, cabbage, onions, green
    peppers, cauliflower.
Chocolate.
Eggs.
Shellfish.
Nuts.
Citrus fruits.
Synthetic vitamins (either mother's or baby's).

If you taste your milk regularly, you may be able to identify which foods change its flavor. Several mothers have told me that they have noticed a change in the taste of their milk after they have indulged in spicy ethnic foods. The taste change also coincided with a colicky period in their babies. The changing taste of breast milk may be one of the ways babies learn to like the strong-flavored foods of their particular culture; they pick up on the flavor of garlic, curry, or chili in the mother's milk.

Smoking
Colic incidence is higher in infants whose mothers smoke (Said 1984). This study also showed a higher incidence of colic when fathers smoked, leading the researchers to conclude that the effects were the result of smoke in the home environment rather than a direct transfer of chemicals through the mothers' milk. Not only are smoking mothers more likely to have colicky babies, but their coping ability may also be lessened. Recent studies have shown that mothers who smoke have lower prolactin levels (Nybor 1984).

Birth and Colic
Events surrounding the birth may affect colic. The incidence of colic is higher in infants who are the product of a complicated and stressful birth and who experienced a lot of mother-baby separation after birth. This goes along with the general tendency for infants to be fussy if they had a rough start and were separated from their mothers.

Another Colic Theory
At this point let me interject my own theory of the cause of colic in some babies. This impression is based upon my experience in pediatric practice and on my review of medical research about colic. Colic is something a baby does, not something he has. It is a behavior, not a disease. I sometimes think we attribute colic to the wrong end of the baby. It seems more like a temperament and neuro-developmental problem than an intestinal problem. I feel the colicky baby belongs to the whole spectrum of fussy or high need babies. They come wired with the supersensitive, intense, disorganized, and slow-to-adapt temperament described in the

profile of the high need baby. Rather than fuss all of the time, the colicky baby concentrates his fussiness toward the end of the day, as if he has stored it all up for the evening blast.

Colic usually does not begin until after the second week of life. Could it be that during this grace period after birth there is something missing in the infant's adjustment to life outside the womb? There is a tendency in our culture to view the newborn as a person separate from the mother, but perhaps the newborn doesn't feel that way. Is it possible that certain high need babies need to be "glued" to their mothers for the first week or two after birth, nursed on demand, carried in arms, nestled next to the mother to sleep, and generally cared for in an organized, predictable, womb-like environment? If these infants do not get what they need and expect, they react with a behavior we call colic, which may be nothing more than the depression and anger of a baby who is not fitting well into his environment. I think that this may be a contributing factor in some, but not all, colicky babies. Even babies who have had the benefit of close attachment parenting from the moment of birth (I call them "right from the start" babies) get colic.

Why Evening Colic?
Another reason why I feel that colic is a neuro-developmental problem or even a hormonal problem is that it occurs most often in the evening hours, from 6:00-9:00 p.m., the time of day some parents refer to as "the pits." If colic were caused by allergies, why would babies show this problem only three hours a day? While no one completely understands why colic occurs mainly in the evenings, there are some possible explanations.

Low parental reserves. Parents' reserves are lowest toward the end of the day. Babies couldn't time their colicky episodes more inconveniently. The colicky baby is upset just when most mothers are least able physically and emotionally to offer comfort. These babies need the most when parents are least able to give. By late afternoon or evening, most mothers are worn out by their babies' incessant demands. Even the most time-honored comforter, mother's breast, may not measure up to expectations at the end of the day. Levels of fat and protein in breast milk are lowest toward evening, and breastfeeding may then be less satisfying for the baby. Many mothers report a diminished milk supply toward the evening. Mothers also experience hormonal changes in the evening. Prolactin, which I call the perseverance hormone, is highest during sleep and in the morning hours. The blood level of cortisone is lowest around 6:00 p.m., though how this affects maternal coping is not known.

Disturbance in biological rhythms.   Colic may be a disturbance in daily biological rhythms. The human body has daily fluctuations in sleep patterns, body temperature, and hormonal concentration. These biological peaks and valleys that occur in every twenty-four hour period are called the circadian rhythm. For example, two important hormones, cortisone and growth hormone, are highest in the early morning hours and lowest in the evening hours. In the first few months of a baby's life, these daily fluctuations are disorganized. By four-to-six months of age, the pattern becomes more like the norm. At the same time, the infant's sleep patterns become better organized, and colic subsides. Coincidence or cause and effect?

Hormonal problems.   Along with a temporary immaturity of biological rhythms, colic may also be the result of hormonal disturbances or immaturity. There may be a deficiency of a hormone which would normally calm the baby toward the end of the day. Excess amounts of another hormone might upset the baby in the evening hours. There are a few studies which lend support to this idea. Progesterone is a hormone which can have calming and sleep-inducing effects. At birth the baby receives progesterone from the placenta. The calming effect of maternal progesterone wears off in a week or two, and colic begins if the infant does not produce enough progesterone on his own. One study showed that colicky infants had low progesterone levels and that colic improved when treated with a progesterone-like drug (Clark 1963). Another study found no difference in progesterone levels in colicky and non-colicky infants (Weissbluth and Green 1983). This author, however, in another study grouped colicky infants together with infants of difficult temperaments or low sensory thresholds and concluded that "plasma progesterone levels were unusually low" in this group (Weissbluth 1983). Breastfed babies in this study had higher levels of progesterone. The significance of this finding is not yet clear, but it may one day help explain why some babies are fussier than others.

Prostaglandins have also recently been implicated in colic. These hormones cause strong contractions of intestinal muscles. In a study in which prostaglandins were used therapeutically to treat heart disease, the two infants involved developed colicky symptoms (Sankaran 1981).

Observations of an increased incidence of colic in infants who were the products of an unusually stressful delivery may also lend support to hormonal theories about the basis of colic, although there is still much to be learned about the effect of birth on the hormonal and behavioral states of the newborn.

Planning Ahead for Evening Colic

I suspect that colic is the result of many causes, temperamental, physiological, and environmental, that overwhelm a baby's immature coping skills. When I witness a colicky episode I can't help but feel that something physical and chemical is going on within that baby. He is not just upset, he hurts! I want to reach for some magic medicine that will bring instant relief to this helpless little person, yet I know full well that I cannot offer treatment if I don't know the cause. In light of present knowledge about colic, the best anyone can do is to comfort the baby and minimize the factors that may contribute to the baby's fussiness.

Plan ahead for evening colic by completing your household duties earlier in the day. Prepare the evening meal in the morning. Parents of colicky babies get used to casseroles that can be made ahead of time. It is wise to find ways to avoid chores and commitments that will sap your energy during those evening colicky times.

Another way to plan ahead for evening colic is to encourage your baby to take a late afternoon nap. Around 4:00 p.m., nestle up to your baby and nurse off to sleep together ("nap nursing"). Late afternoon napping and nursing helps both mother and baby: mother gets a rest, a boost in her prolactin levels, and an energy recharge in preparation for the evening colic; baby's system also gets a rest at this crucial time before the colic begins. Some mothers report that this late afternoon quiet time minimizes the frequency and severity of the evening colic.

When Will It Stop?
Colic begins around two weeks of age, peaks in severity between six and eight weeks, and is usually over by six months. In a study of one hundred colicky infants, the colic had disappeared in fifty percent by three months and in ninety percent by six months. In only one percent of these babies did the colic last until one year of age (Wessel 1954). In England, Illingworth (1954) studied fifty cases of evening colic and found that it disappeared in eighty-five percent of the babies by three months and disappeared in all of them by four months. Colic that persists beyond three to four months is likely to be caused by a medical problem such as a milk intolerance.

Colic is at its worst at the period of an infant's development when he can do the least to comfort and amuse himself. During the first three months, babies are almost totally dependent on caregivers for stimulation. The severity of colic seems to lessen at a rate similar to the infant's development. I feel that the reason colic begins to subside around three months is that babies of that age can finally see clearly and are attracted by the visual delights and distractions around them. They can begin to do things with their hands and are learning self-soothing techniques such as finger-sucking, eye contact, and waving their arms and legs to let off steam. Around three months most babies show an increased maturity of the central nervous system, revealed by gradual organization of their sleep patterns. Also by the time the baby is two to three months old, most parents have become more adept at soothing techniques. But even though severe evening colicky episodes usually subside by six months, the general behavioral traits of the high need baby may persist.

How many babies have colic? It is difficult to assess the true incidence of colic since only the parents can tell the story. Most studies claim that from twelve to sixteen percent of all babies experience some colic episodes during the first six months. The incidence of both colicky and fussy babies (babies who cry a lot) is around twenty-five percent.

Colic Communication Tips

Since most colic occurs outside of doctors' office hours, most baby doctors do not have the privilege of witnessing a colic attack. When seeking professional help for your colicky or fussy baby, be honest with your doctor about two important points: how much the colic bothers your baby and how much it bothers you.

Here are some of the things you'll need to tell the doctor when discussing your baby's colic problems. Think about them ahead of time, and make a list to take with you to the doctor's office.

When the colic episodes started, how often they occur, how long they last.

The time of day and the circumstances around which they occur (at home, with caregivers other than mother, when the family is busy).

What seems to turn the colic episodes on and what turns them off.

Where you feel the baby's pain is coming from, what his face, abdomen, and extremities look like.

A description of the cry.

Details about feeding: breast or bottle, frequency,
   swallowing. Do you hear the baby gulping air?
Nature of the baby's bowel movements: easy or
   straining, soft or hard, how frequent.
How much he passes gas.
Spitting up: how often, how soon after feeding, how
   much force.
What the baby's bottom looks like. A persistent diaper rash or a red, burnt-looking bottom suggests
   some sort of food intolerance.
What you have tried to do for the colic episodes—
   what worked and what didn't.
What your diagnosis is.

Be sure to tell your doctor what effect the colic is having
on the whole family. I have discovered that it is not uncom-
mon for mothers to open a conversation by telling me, "Our
whole family is falling apart—me, my baby, and my marriage."
Don't hesitate to let yourself go during the office visit. This
gets the point across that your baby's colic bothers you.

If your doctor is unable to witness one of these colicky
episodes, it may help to make a "distress tape," a recording
of one of the baby's crying jags. I find it difficult, though,
to truly appreciate an infant's cry from the sound only; there
is so much that body language can tell you about the level
of the baby's distress. If you really want to get the point across
and you have the equipment (or can rent it) have your husband make a video tape of you and your baby during a colicky episode so that your counselor can truly witness a
mother-infant pair in distress. Some parents find it very ther-
apeutic to sit back and analyze a series of tapes of crying
episodes as their infant grows older. When they look back,
parents are often amazed at the complete turnabout in the
baby's personality. As they look at or listen to some of the
earlier distress tapes they often exclaim, "We've come a long
way, baby!"

I find it particularly helpful to have parents keep some
sort of a diary that lists the activity of the infant on one side

of the page and the time of day and the activity of the rest of the family on the other. You'll be surprised at correlations you'll discover. For example, I found that typical colic seldom awakens the baby during the night. Pain that awakens babies from sleep is more likely to have a physical than an emotional cause.

If possible, both mother and father should attend the office visit. The presence of the father keeps mother honest. Mothers may sometimes play down how much their crying baby upsets them; they fear that such a revelation will shatter their perfect mother image in the eyes of the pediatrician. Fathers also may more readily volunteer how the fussy baby is affecting the overall dynamics of the family. One family came in for colic counseling with me, and I really didn't appreciate the severity of the problem until the father volunteered, "I had a vasectomy last week. We'll never go through this again." I got the picture.

What Your Doctor's Looking For
Communicating all of the above information helps your doctor to detect any possible hidden medical causes of your baby's crying episodes. Having all the facts makes it easier to track down possible sources of your baby's discomfort.

Ear infections. The symptoms of ear infections are frequently missed in colicky babies because they're passed off as another instance of "there he goes again." Keep in mind that most true colic does not awaken babies from sleep; ear infections do. In fact, they are worse at night because when a baby lies flat the infected fluid presses down on the sensitive eardrum. A baby who seems in pain when lying down but not when sitting up may have an ear infection. Cold symptoms such as a snotty nose, draining eyes, and a low grade fever often accompany the infection. Be aware of signs of a perforated eardrum: Baby suddenly wakes up screaming during the night and then toward the morning seems better, but you notice some yellowish-white crusty fluid around the outside of the ear. The baby may seem more comfortable after the eardrum has perforated because the pressure is released, but you should still obtain medical attention. Remember that babies with ear infections often seem better the next morning because they are no longer lying down.

Diaper rash.   Sudden outbursts of screaming may be caused by a sore bottom. The type of diaper rashes that are particularly distressing are the burnt, red, raw rashes caused by acid stools during diarrhea. A baking soda bath (one tablespoon baking soda into a couple inches of water in baby's bathtub) may soothe the diaper rash caused by acid stools.

Urinary tract infections.   The most serious hidden cause of colic is urinary tract infection. These infections are subtle. They do not begin as quickly and severely as ear infections and can last several weeks before they are detected. Urinary tract infections can cause kidney damage if undetected and untreated. I believe that all fussy, colicky babies should have at least three urinalyses. When making your appointment for a fussy baby consultation, ask the doctor's assistant to mail you three urine bags so that you can bring in urine specimens on or before the day of your appointment.

Calming the Colicky Baby

The Colic Dance
Imagine ten mothers or fathers with colicky babies all dancing around at once, trying to soothe their little ones. One by one the tense babies drift off to sleep and melt into the arms of the parent. Every mother and father who has coped with a colicky baby has developed a unique rhythm, a dance motivated by love and desperation that keeps going until either the crier or the dancer wears down.

While each dance movement is as unique as a fingerprint, there are some common elements I have observed among all experienced dancers. They hold the baby firmly with a relaxed "I'm in charge" grasp and with as much skin-to-skin contact as possible. Nestled against mother's breast is usually the favorite embrace, but father's chest may provide an interesting change (which I call the warm fuzzy).

The rhythm of the dance usually oscillates gently back and forth, alternating side-to-side and up-and-down motions. There's a lot of bending and straightening of the knees. The most successful rhythms are around seventy beats per minute (which corresponds to the pulse of uterine blood flow which the unborn baby has grown accustomed to). Gentle humming usually accompanies this dance; it sounds as if the mother is trying to approximate as closely as possible the sounds of the womb.

Fathers are particularly adept at developing their own type of colic carry. The one that has worked best for me is to drape the baby stomach down over my forearm, her head in the crook of my elbow and legs straddling my hand. I grasp the diaper area firmly and my forearm presses on the baby's tense abdomen. The "warm fuzzy" position that I particu-

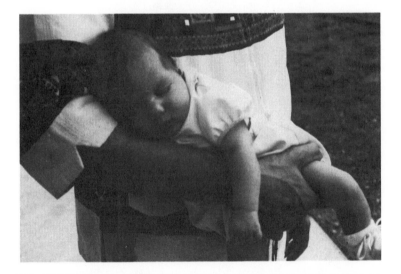

*Draping the baby over dad's forearm helps
to relax a tense, colicky tummy.*

larly enjoy is to lie down and hold our baby securely with her head snuggled in my left armpit, her ear over my heart-beat, and her cheek on my chest. The rhythm of the heart-beat plus the breathing movements will usually lull baby to sleep.

Another favorite snuggle is to dance neck-to-cheek. The baby snuggles her cheek into the groove between my jaw and shoulder. In this position baby not only hears my hum-ming close to her ear but also feels the sound vibrations from my jawbone all over her skull.

Some babies prefer a lot of eye contact as you sing to them. Your baby may like to be held about a foot away from your face with one hand firmly under his bottom and the other firmly on his back. You can then bounce him rhythmically—fast or slow, hard or smoothly. This is a good

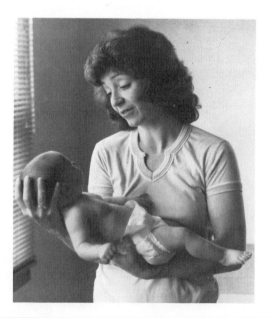

Holding the baby away from you adds eye contact as well as motion to your colic dance.

way to get the baby to stop crying before going on to his favorite snuggling position. It is especially effective if you can make eye contact and croon baby's name. Don't feel destroyed if occasionally your baby does not respond to your comforting dance yet responds when an experienced friend cuts in. Some experienced grandmothers have a very calming way of moving with babies.

You can even develop a colic dance with your unborn baby. Some mothers of large families can often predict the temperament of a baby by activity in the womb. Mothers who have calmed their agitated unborn babies by songs and dances during pregnancy find that the same songs and dances work after birth.

Abdominal Relaxation Techniques

Sometimes warmth and gentle pressure on the abdomen helps soothe a colicky baby. Place baby tummy down on a half-filled warm water bottle that you have covered with a towel to protect the baby's skin. Letting baby fall asleep stomach down on a cushion with his legs dangling over the edge causes some soothing pressure to be applied to his belly. Some babies enjoy dad's large, warm hand pressing gently on their tummies; the palm should be over the navel and the fingers and thumb encircle baby's abdomen. Sometimes inserting a glycerin suppository into the baby's rectum with one hand while kneading baby's abdomen with the other will decompress a gas-filled abdomen.

Massaging baby's stomach.   Infant massage is becoming quite an art among mothers of colicky babies. Here is a technique we have used in our babies.

Imagine a large ''U'' upside down on the baby's abdomen. This is the large intestine or colon along which the gas must pass, beginning on baby's right (your left), moving across his middle and down his left side until it exits through the rectum. By firmly and deeply massaging with your flattened fingers in a circular motion you can move gas pockets along this path. You can use the "I love you" method: Start with a single downward stroke for the "I" on baby's left side (see figure). This will move gas down and out of the last one-third of the colon. Then do the upside down "L" (the numeral 7 as you look at it) for the "love," moving gas along the middle segment and down the baby's left side. Finally, do the whole upside down "U" for the "you" as you stroke again along the baby's right side across the middle segment, and down the left side. Baby must be relaxed for this massage to work, as a tense abdomen will resist the motion of your hands. Try it in a warm bath together or after some other comforting treatments. Warm oil on your hands will make massage easier.

The bubble bath.   Use the abdominal massage technique while immersing your baby's tummy in warm water. As baby passes the gas, bubbles will appear in the water.

Lay baby belly down.   Tiny infants sleep better, cry less, and spit up less when placed in the prone position. Researchers have shown that the body seems to relax more in the belly-down position. The heart and breathing rates are also slower.

The "I love you" massage helps move gas through baby's abdomen.

Pacifiers

A general guideline for comforting the colicky baby would state that if it's safe and it works, use it. This is especially true with pacifiers, after the first month or so when nipple confusion is no longer a problem. (A pacifier nipple requires a different sucking action than mother's breast; this can confuse a tiny infant and contribute to problems with breast-feeding.) Some fussy babies need a large amount of non-nutritive sucking, and a pacifier fills the bill. Beware of

---

More Massage Techniques

"I tried warm baths with my baby. This helped, but only as long as he was immersed in the warm water, and realistically, you can't spend your life in a bath! I also massaged his tummy while he was in the water. With his feet toward me, I would place my left hand across his middle and knead rather deeply with my fingers concentrating on his left side close to the rib cage. This helped some, but he only liked it when he was in the water. After his bath I would rub him with lotion, starting with his precious little feet and working up each leg. I found when I reached his thighs his wails immediately turned into cackles of laughter. I began to concentrate on massaging his thighs when the colicky periods began, and even without the bath, the reaction was always the same.

"The thigh massage I found most helpful went like this. I would lay Eric in my lap on his back with his head on my knee and his feet at my stomach. I would place a hand on each thigh, thumb in the groin area and fingers on the outside of the leg. Then I would use a rather firm deep kneading motion with equal pressure on both the inside and the outside of the leg, squeezing, rolling, then releasing. It worked every time, turning those pitiful wails into laughter—at least for a while!"

using the pacifier as a mother substitute. The other end of a pacifier should always be attached to a person. A breast or a finger makes the best pacifier.

Table I

Instructions to parents of infants in treatment group I.
  When infant crying continues despite all efforts to stop it, including feeding, do the following:
1. Put the baby in the crib and let him cry for up to a half hour.
2. If still crying, pick the baby up for a minute or so to calm him. Then return him to the crib.
3. Repeat the above until the infant falls asleep or three hours have passed.
4. After three hours the baby should be fed.

Table II

Instructions to parents of infants in treatment group II
1. Try to never let your baby cry.
2. In attempting to discover why your infant is crying consider these possibilities:
    a. The baby is hungry and wants to be fed.
    b. The baby wants to suck, although he is not hungry.
    c. The baby wants to be held.
    d. The baby is bored and wants stimulation.
    e. The baby is tired and wants to sleep.
3. If the crying continues for more than five minutes with one response, then try another.
4. Decide on your own in what order to explore the above possibilities.
5. Don't be concerned about overfeeding your baby. This will not happen.
6. Don't be concerned about spoiling your baby. This also will not happen.

Respond Promptly to Baby's Crying

In my experience the more promptly the cries of a colicky infant are attended to, the less he cries. The myth that parental overresponsiveness can reinforce the crying and produce so-called "trained crying" is erroneous. Both the experience of mothers and scientific studies have shown this theory to be false (Bell and Ainsworth 1972).

A recent study showed that parental responsiveness can lessen the severity of colic (Taubman 1984). This study compared thirty colicky babies with thirty non-colicky babies. The colicky babies were divided into two groups. Parents in Group One were advised to use a restrained response to their infants, as characterized by the behaviors listed in Table 1. This advice was based on the hypothesis that babies cry no matter what the parents do and that overstimulation contributes to excessive crying. Group Two parents were advised to make immediate efforts to stop the crying (see Table 2); this advice assumed that infants cry to express a desire and they will continue to cry until the desire is met. The study found that colicky infants cried an average of 2.6 ($\pm$ 1.0) hours per day, compared with 1.0 ($\pm$ 0.5) hour per day for non-colicky infants. In other words, colicky babies cried more than twice as much as non-colicky babies. After treatment with the restrained approach, the infants in Group One showed no decrease in daily crying time. After treatment with the responsive approach, the infants in Group Two cried seventy percent less. The crying decreased from 2.6 hours to 0.8 hours per day. It appears that a responsive parent-infant relationship can lessen colicky behavior in some infants.

Medical Treatment of Colic

In my experience, drug treatment of colic fails more often than it works but there are some infants who are significantly helped by medication. **Check with your doctor before giving your baby any medication for colic.**

Antispasmodics. Medicines such as the prescription drug dicyclomine relax the smooth muscle of the intestines. One-half to one teaspoon of this syrup given a half-hour before the evening feeding or around the time the colic episodes usually occur may offer some relief.

Antiflatulents. Simethicone drops (also a prescription drug) may offer some relief from gas pains. These agents work by lessening the formation of gas in the intestines. Acidophilus, which is basically a yogurt culture, also seems to lessen intestinal gas. It is available in liquid form in health food stores. Give baby a dose of one milliliter with feedings during the colicky times of the day.

Herbal Teas. Chamomile and fennel sometimes have a soothing effect on babies. Place one-half teaspoon of tea in a pot with one cup of boiling water. Cover and steep for five to ten minutes. A few teaspoons of this warm tea may help baby feel better.

If the baby's fussiness is true colic, the antispasmodics or the antiflatulents are the only prescription medications that seem to work. I don't advise using sedatives such as phenobarbitol. Not only are they usually ineffective in true colic, but also they occasionally have a paradoxical effect and make a fussy baby even fussier. Anticholinergic drugs (drugs which contain belladonna) are also advertised for colic, but both their safety and effectiveness are questionable. Drugs containing sedatives and/or anticholinergics are classified in the unproven category in relation to colic by the FDA. This means that comparison studies and true scientific evaluations are lacking for the application of these drugs in colic. Parents should also bear in mind that drugs given in the form of an elixir contain a high alcohol content; fifteen to twenty percent of the syrup may be alcohol.

Caution. Beware of colic remedies which have not been proven to be both safe and effective. For example there has been one death and one near-death from the high potassium levels in a colic remedy, a salt substitute, proposed in the book *Let's Have Healthy Children*.

Other helpful remedies. A baby-sized glycerin rectal suppository may help expel some stool and gas during a straining episode or if baby is constipated. These suppositories resemble tiny rocket ships. Insert the suppository an inch or so into the rectum and hold baby's buttocks together a few minutes to allow the suppository to dissolve.

The most effective "medicine" for soothing the fussy baby comes out of the parent's heart, not out of the drugstore. It is wise to consider colic not as a disease to be treated but as a person to be comforted.

References
American Academy of Pediatrics Committee on Nutrition. 1983. Soy-protein formulas: recommendations for use in infant feeding. *Pediatrics* 72:359.

Anderson, G. C. 1983. Infant colic: a possible solution. *MCN* 8:185.

Bell and Ainsworth. 1972. Infant crying and maternal responsiveness. *Child Develop* 43:1171.

Brennemann, J. 1940. *Practice of Pediatrics*, vol. 1. New York: W. F. Prior Co.

Carey, W. B. 1968. Maternal anxiety and infantile colic: is there a relationship? *Clin Pediatr* 7:590.

Clark, R. L. et al. 1963. A study of the possible relationship of progesterone to colic. *Pediatrics* 31:65.

Evans, R. W. et al. 1981. Maternal diet and infantile colic in breast-fed infants. *Lancet* 1:1340.

Illingworth, R. S. 1954. Three month colic. *Arch Dis Child* 29:165.

Jakobsson, I. and Lindberg, T. 1983. Cow's milk proteins cause infantile colic in breastfed infants: a double blind study. *Pediatrics* 71:268.

Jorup, S. 1952. Colonic hyperperistalis in neurolabile infants. *Acta Paediatr Scand* (suppl) 85:1.

Liebman, W. M. 1981. Infantile colic: association with lactose and milk intolerance. *J Am Med Assoc* 245:732.

Lothe, L. et al. 1982. Cow's milk formula as a cause of infantile colic: a double blind study. *Pediatrics* 70:7.

Nybor, A. et al. 1984. Suppressed prolactin levels in cigarette smoking breastfeeding women. *Clin Endocrinol* 17:363.

Paradise, J. L. 1966. Maternal and other factors in the etiology of infantile colic. *J Am Med Assoc* 197:123.

Said, G. et al. 1984. Infantile colic and parental smoking. *Br Med J* 289:660.

Sankaran, K. et. al. 1981. Intestinal colic and diarrhea as side effects of intravenous alprostadil administration. *Am J Dis Child* 135:664.

Sears, W. 1982. *Creative Parenting*. New York: Dodd Mead.

Taubman, B. 1984. Clinical trial of the treatment of colic by modification of parent-infant interaction. *Pediatrics* 74:998.

Weissbluth, M. 1983. *Crybabies*. New York: Arbor House.

Weissbluth, M. and Green, O. 1983. Plasma progesterone concentrations in infants: relation to infantile colic. *J Pediatr* 103:935.

Wessel, M. A. et. al. 1954. Paroxysmal fussing in infancy, sometimes called colic. *Pediatrics* 14:421.

CHAPTER 6

Soothing the Fussy Baby

"No one thing works all the time," complained a creative father who had collected a large repertoire of soothing techniques. In this chapter I will share with you techniques that have worked in our own family and the many ideas which parents have related to me over the years.

Soothing techniques can be grouped into three general categories:

1. Rhythmic motion.

2. Physical contact.

3. Soothing sounds.

Soothing the fussy baby is basically a matter of using "back to the womb" activities. Picture the fetus's womb environment. He is in a free-floating fluid environment with which every point of his body is in contact; the fluid is at a constant temperature. His hunger is automatically and continuously satisfied, and the sounds around him are melodious, calming, and rhythmic. Even when temporarily upset by his mother's anxieties or loud noises from the outside world, the fetus has the reassurance that his tranquil world will soon return to its usual predictability. The unborn baby gets accustomed to feeling right. Soothing techniques are all aimed at duplicating, as much as possible, the creature comforts that the baby has been programmed prenatally to expect from his environment. If you have a high need baby, you might consider the first three months after birth to be a fourth trimester of your pregnancy.

Moving in Harmony with Your Baby

Why Motion Is Important to Babies

Behind each ear is a tiny organ of balance called the vestibular system. This intricate system helps various parts of the body become aware of their relation to other parts and helps the body as a whole balance in space. The vestibular system is like three tiny carpenter's levels, one oriented for side-to-side balance, another for up-and-down, and the third for back-and-forth. They all function together to keep the body in balance. Every time you move, the fluid in these levels moves against tiny hair-like filaments which vibrate and send nerve impulses to the muscles in your body that will keep you in balance. For example, if you lean over too far to one side the vestibular system signals that you should lean back to the other side to stay in balance. The unborn baby has a very sensitive vestibular system which is constantly stimulated because the fetus is in almost continuous motion. This is why motion, not stillness, is the normal state for a baby; a baby is born programmed to expect a stimulated vestibular system. The picture book baby lying quietly but alertly in his crib is a totally unrealistic expectation of how babies behave. The unborn baby also may not be accustomed to changes in gravity. This may explain why ultrasensitive babies have to be put down very slowly.

How to Move with Your Baby

Because a newborn baby's vestibular system is accustomed to constant stimulation in three dimensions, the ideal rocking motion for soothing a fussy baby contains movements in all three planes, side to side, back and forth, and up and down. Rocking in a rocking chair may soothe some babies, but it only stimulates the vestibular system in one plane, back and forth (with a small amount of up-and-down motion). Soothing fussy babies usually requires motion in all three planes. Experienced baby comforters have recognized this and developed a **colic dance** which goes something like this: With the baby in a sling or baby carrier, draped over your shoulder, or swaddled or nestled in your arms, you begin to walk, swaying from side to side (thus stimulating the side-to-side portion of the baby's vestibular system). After every few steps you bend back and forth, balancing on one foot while swinging the other foot forward. The third part of this little dance is the up-and-down motion, accomplished most easily with a heel-toe type of walk. You spring upward on the ball of your foot just until you feel a little bit of pulling in your calf muscles. It is more appropriate for a mother to say that she "dances with her baby" to comfort him rather than to say simply that she walks with the baby. This dance causes all three areas of the baby's vestibular system to be stimulated.

Research has shown that most infants are soothed best by the up-and-down motion of the dance. Some babies with average levels of soothability are calmed simply by being carried in the parent's arms and walked with; that is the level of motion the unborn baby has been most accustomed to. The side-to-side swaying action is more natural for most parents than the up-and-down and back-and-forth movements. This is why you will very often see an experienced mother or father standing with feet planted on the ground but the rest of the body swaying from side to side while holding a sleeping baby. He or she is hoping that the motion will keep the baby asleep, especially at certain events where being a baby, let alone a crying baby, is not socially acceptable. In fact, parents do so much moving around during the first few months after birth that swaying back and forth becomes a way of life. A mother told me once that as she was standing at a party holding a glass of ginger ale, another mother came up and commented on the fact that she seemed to be teetering back and forth a bit. This observer then exclaimed, "I know you haven't had too much to drink, so I guess you must have just had a new baby."

Nursing on the move.   A very effective soothing technique is to feed your baby while standing and swaying rhythmically from side to side or while rocking in a chair.

Baby's favorite dancing partner.   Ever wonder why in some cases only the mother can soothe the baby? High need babies are highly selective. Oftentimes only the mother can develop the proper soothing dance because she's the person who has been in motion with the baby for the previous nine months. It's as if the baby says to the mother, "I like your style." This also explains the frustration that some fathers discover when they try to give their wives some relief by calming a fussy baby. The dance with the flailing, upset baby ends after a few minutes with "Here, you take him. I give up."

Fathers, take heart. Your baby is not rejecting you; he just hasn't grown accustomed to your style. The two of you haven't been dancing together for nine months, the way a mother and baby have. There will be times when an upset baby prefers a father's calm firm arms to the mother's tense ones which are tired out by a whole day of coping.

Speed.   How fast to rock? Studies have shown that babies are soothed most quickly by rocking done at a frequency of sixty to seventy cycles per minute. Isn't it interesting that this corresponds to the average rate of a mother's heartbeat and the average rhythm of walking? This further supports the concept that an infant is calmed best by duplicating the sound and motion he became accustomed to in the womb.

When the "Womb" Wears Out

Soothing your baby with motion means you have to create the feeling that he is back in the womb. However, sooner or later your arms and legs get tired and the "womb" wears out. The following are some helpful hints that will keep the womb feeling going, even if mother or father is getting tired.

Slings

There are a myriad of baby carriers on the market, all designed to keep parent and baby close to each other. I have had experience with the following commercially available carriers in my family and in my practice, and I'm happy to recommend them: Baby Matey (a Canadian carrier), Gerry Carrier, Happy Family Baby Carrier, Sara's Ride (for babies over three months), Snugli, and Strolee. You can also make your own baby carrier or tie the baby into a traditional sling or shawl. Patterns and instructions are available in La Leche League International's *Baby Carrier Packet*.

"Wearing" your fussy baby in a carrier keeps the womb feeling going with gentle motion and physical closeness.

Using a variety of slings and carriers to keep your baby in contact with you is known as **marsupial mothering**, a term derived from kangaroos and other similar mammals who keep their babies close to them in external pouches after they are born. If you are blessed with a high need baby you'll find it helpful simply to get used to "wearing" your baby.

Swings

Placing a fussy baby in a mechanical swing will often calm him and give parents a few minutes of much needed rest. These devices are usually set to swing at around sixty beats per minute. The newer models may even provide an accompanying lullaby. Soothing babies has now become big business. Commercial swings include the Swyngomatic, the Strolee, and the Century.

Some babies will not settle in swings. The reason is that swings provide motion in only two planes, back and forth and slightly up and down. Some high need babies are so selective that they will not calm down unless that third motion of swaying from side to side is added. This may be why some homemade swings work better than commercial ones, as long as the baby has good head control (usually by four months). While the commercially available swings are hemmed in on both sides by the stand, homemade swings dangle from a door frame or a backyard tree or post and create motion in all three directions. The homemade swings allow a wider and more circular motion which may work better. Some babies may protest in swings that sway because they feel dizzy.

Other Motion Sources

Car rides.   One successful technique for calming fussy babies and inducing sleep is what I call **freeway therapy**. Place baby in an approved car seat and take a ride. Rides on the freeway are the most effective; stopping and starting may awaken a sensitive baby who needs continuous monotonous movement. This technique is also called *freeway fathering* because it is particularly useful for fathers who wish to give mom a break but discover that the baby will not settle dancing in dad's arms. This car ride can also be a family time when mom and dad turn on some music, dad drives, mom rests, and the two parents have some uninterrupted communication while the baby sleeps. Driving for at least twenty minutes after the baby nods off allows him to enter the phase of deep sleep. You can then return home and pick up both the baby and the car seat and allow him to finish his nap still in the car seat. If even this wakes him up and you, too, are desperate for sleep, stretch out in the car yourself and have a nap. Keep a pillow in the car just in case.

Trampolines. A father of a high need baby recently told me that he is able to calm his baby by dancing rhythmically on a small home trampoline. This certainly makes sense in light of babies' need for stimulation in all three planes of motion. Dancing on a trampoline would allow dad to exaggerate the up-and-down, back-and-forth, and side-to-side movements. Chalk up another one for creative parents.

Baby carriages. Get an old-fashioned tub-like carriage with lots of springs, the type called a pram that bounces a lot. Gentle bouncing in these well-padded prams often works much better in soothing the baby than the new, collapsible, springless baby carriages. If you use a stroller, find one in which baby faces you.

Moving attractions. Things that move rhythmically and have a consistent, monotonous sound often soothe a fussy baby:

Revolving ceiling fan.
Shower. (Place baby in an infant seat in the bathroom while you take a shower.)
Waves on a beach.
Waterfalls.
Pendulum of a grandfather clock.
Trees swaying in the wind. (Place baby in front of a window to gaze at them.)

Physical Contact: Getting in Touch with Your Baby

Holding your baby close to you is an effective soothing technique. Babies want to feel close to some*body*, with as much skin-to-skin contact as possible.

A Warm Bath Together

Fill the tub at least half full. Mother lies down in the tub holding the baby (or dad can hand mom the baby). Let baby half float while nursing, your breasts being just a few inches above the water line. Leave the faucet running and the tub's drain open just a bit. This not only provides the soothing sound of running water; it also keeps the water at a comfortable temperature (around 100° Fahrenheit).

A Warm Fuzzy

Drape the bare-skinned but diapered baby over daddy's chest. Place baby's ear over daddy's heartbeat. Dad's heartbeat combined with the rhythm of his breathing movements plus firm rhythmic patting on the baby's back will usually

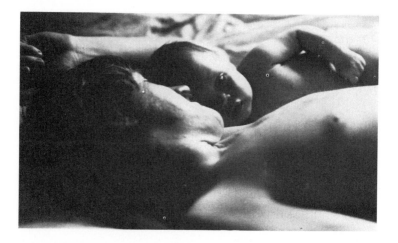

Skin-to-skin contact along with the sound of dad's heartbeat and his breathing movements will soothe a fussy baby.

soothe both members of this couple to sleep. In my experience, the **warm fuzzy** works best in the first three months; older babies squirm too much to lie quietly on dad's chest.

Baby Massage
Massaging your baby will help him relax and calm down. Several books, including Dr. Frederick Leboyer's *Loving Hands*, give instructions for massaging your baby. You'll find more about baby massage in the previous chapter.

Nestle Nursing
When baby is tired, lie down together and curl up womb-like around your baby, letting him snuggle close within your arms and breasts with as much skin-to-skin contact as possible. You can both nurse off to sleep this way.

A Waterbed and Lambskin
Lambskin mats and waterbeds have been effective at soothing some babies. Lambskins have been specially shorn to be both safe and comfortable for babies as well as machine washable. Drape the lambskin on your waterbed, and place baby tummy down on the lambskin. The combination of the touch of the lambskin, the patting of your hand, and the rhythmic motion of the waterbed may soothe baby off to sleep. When creating a wave motion in the waterbed push down on the mattress sixty to seventy times per minute; this is the rhythm baby is used to.

Bending Your Baby
Some high need babies tend to stiffen out their muscles and arch their backs. They are difficult to hold still because they don't cuddle easily. You can relax this kind of baby by carrying him in a bent forward position. When you bend baby's hips and legs, he tends to relax his entire back, becoming less of an "archer," especially during feeding. Pumping baby's legs ("bicycling") may also help. Draping baby over a beach ball is another way to untense him. Many babies think this is a lot of fun.

Sounds That Soothe

Another group of gentling techniques uses various calming sounds to soothe the fussy baby. While some of the following suggestions may seem a bit unusual, they do work. Remember that babies are accustomed to sounds at a tempo resembling heartbeats, between sixty and seventy beats per minute, so if you can adjust the speed of the sound, do so. Here are some suggestions for soothing sounds:

A metronome.

A loud grandfather clock. (Turn the chimes off.)

Records of mothers' heartbeats and other recordings of womb sounds.

Running water from a faucet or shower.

The whirring hum of the vacuum cleaner, air conditioner, fan, dishwasher.

Tape recordings of ocean waves, waterfalls, rainfall.

Bending a baby at the hips counteracts the tendency to arch the back and stiffen the legs.

Mother or father singing lullabies, live or on tape (the lower, more monotonous, and more rhythmical the tone, the more soothing).

Tape recordings of baby's own cry. (Played during crying episodes these can startle a baby into silence, giving you a chance to apply other comforting measures.)

Classical music, for example, Mozart, Vivaldi, classical guitar, flute.

"White noise" works best to lull babies to sleep. This is the type of noise that is repetitive and monotonous and involves all the frequencies audible to the human ear. It has no message and lulls the mind into oblivion. Once you have found which types of white noise soothe your baby, make tape recordings of these sounds and play them on a tape recorder that has a continuous playback. One mother I know went through several vacuum cleaners before she realized that she could accomplish the same result by tape recording the vacuum cleaner sound.

Babies settle best to the tune of low, rhythmical lullabies.

You'll discover more methods of soothing your particular fussy baby. One mother of a high need baby who was becoming desperate in her search for a way to quiet her baby shared the following unusual and ingenious technique with me. She strapped her baby into a car seat or infant seat and strapped the seat on top of the washing machine while it was running. The humming and whirring vibrations of the machine lulled the baby to sleep. Perhaps automatic washing machines ought to include a cycle called "wash and sleep."

Sounds that soothe, dances that delight, and cuddles that comfort are all creative gentling techniques that bring out the best in parents and baby.

CHAPTER 7

Feeding the Fussy Baby

During the first few months you will probably spend more time feeding your baby than in any other mother-baby interaction. Fussy babies, however, tend to be fussy feeders, and this can make feeding time difficult. This chapter will help you enjoy your baby's feeding times by making them easier for both of you.

Breast or Bottle: Does It Make a Difference?

Breastfeeding is clearly better for fussy babies—and for their mothers. Because fussiness causes distress in both the baby and his mother, I feel that survival advice should be directed at both. Breastfeeding is designed to help both mother and baby feel better.

Advantages for Fussy Babies

Fewer Allergies.   Breastfeeding eliminates the possibility of milk allergy, one cause of the fussy and colicky baby. Some babies are allergic to the proteins or cannot tolerate the lactose in cow's milk. Cow's milk proteins may cause allergic reactions and an overall unwell feeling. Lactose intolerance is rarely a problem in breastfed babies. Breast milk is a living substance and contains the enzyme lactase which helps babies digest lactose. The lactase in cow's milk formulas has been destroyed by processing. Undigested lactose can ferment in the intestines and cause excess gas which contributes to colicky intestinal pains. Undigested milk products, especially lactose, can also form acid stools which burn baby's bottom and further contribute to fussiness.

More contact with mother.   Because breast milk is digested more rapidly than formula, breastfed babies need to be fed more often. This means they also get held more often. Fussy babies usually need more holding, and the breastfeeding relationship naturally provides them with extra skin-to-skin contact.

What's in It for Mother?
Breastfeeding really pays off for mothers of fussy babies. A mother may be tempted to consider breastfeeding a fussy baby as too draining or too demanding. Many people overlook the fact that breastfeeding actually does something for the mother. Mothers of fussy babies feel that they are constantly giving to the baby, but a breastfeeding baby gives something back to the mother. Breastfeeding increases the mother's level of prolactin, the perseverance hormone. This hormone gives the mother an added boost during those trying times. Many mothers report that breastfeeding has a calming effect on themselves as well as their babies. Hormonal changes are probably responsible for this tranquilizing effect in the mother. There may also be substances in breast

milk that have not yet been identified which have a tranquilizing effect on the baby. In fact, researchers have recently found
a sleep-inducing protein in mother's milk.

The act of breastfeeding forces a mother to relax. It forces
her to put aside other obligations. A breastfeeding mother
can seldom ignore her baby. Breastfeeding mothers often
show a greater sensitivity to their babies' crying. A baby's
cry stimulates blood flow in the mother's breast which is accompanied by the urge to pick up the baby and nurse. Bottle feeding mothers may experience this same hormonal
sensitivity, but they do not follow through on the natural instincts of their bodies—a situation which may cause some
internal confusion in the mother.

Substances in Breast Milk That Cause Fussiness

Although breastfeeding itself has a soothing effect on high
need babies, substances from the mother's diet which enter
breast milk may cause babies to fuss. Cow's milk in a mother's
diet may cause fussy symptoms in her baby. Small amounts
of cow's milk protein may pass into a mother's milk and can
cause allergic reactions in some babies. Sometimes only large
amounts of milk the mother drinks as a beverage will affect
the baby; the mother finds she can eat milk products such
as yogurt and cottage chese without any effect on the baby.
Other babies may be bothered by any amount of milk or
milk product in the mother's diet. With proper nutritional
advice, you might try avoiding milk products for a week to
see if your infant's colic symptoms decrease or disappear.
Keep a careful record of what you eat and of your baby's
fussy spells to help you determine if there is a connection.
Then reintroduce milk into your diet to see if symptoms re-
appear. If you're uncertain of the results, repeat the challenge
test a second time. If your baby's symptoms recur, he is probably sensitive to cow's milk proteins, and you would be wise
to avoid cow's milk while you are nursing him.

Caffeine-containing substances in your diet may also
bother your baby. These include coffee, tea, chocolate, colas,

and some other soft drinks. Many over-the-counter medications also contain caffeine; check the label carefully if you or your baby is caffeine-sensitive.

Gassy foods (for example, raw cabbage, onions, cauliflower, green peppers, and broccoli) have also been implicated in colic. It is difficult to explain scientifically how gassy foods in the mother's diet cause gas in a baby, but who am I to argue with experienced mothers who claim this actually does happen?

On the whole, foods that breastfeeding mothers eat seldom bother most babies. If you're accustomed to tasting your milk, you may be able to detect when it takes on a different taste or smell. This can be a clue to understanding what's going on if your baby suddenly refuses the breast. Decongestants, caffeine-containing cold tablets, oral contraceptives, and prenatal vitamins are among the more common medications that may cause a change in your breast milk and upset your baby.

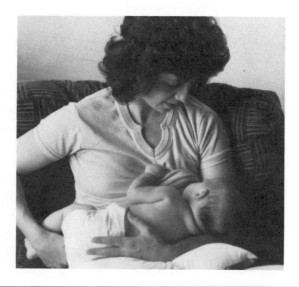

Proper positioning—tummy to tummy with the baby bent around mother's waist—makes it easier to breastfeed the fussy baby.

Breastfeeding Difficulties

It is important to correct breastfeeding difficulties early, especially in high need babies. Breastfeeding is one of your most reliable comforting measures. It is important that you and baby get off to the right start. Babies who have difficulty breastfeeding may develop an unhealthy attitude towards nursing. The baby becomes programmed to fuss as soon as you start to nurse. A La Leche League Leader or a trained lactation specialist can help you correct these difficulties early in your baby's life.

Positioning the Fussy Baby

"It's just the nature of the little beast," a mother lamented humorously as she tried to hang on to her squirming, arching, fussy baby who was pulling away from the breast. Fussy babies are not noted for their mealtime manners. They're inclined to throw their heads backwards and arch their backs; this can make breastfeeding difficult. When a baby arches his back and retracts his head, he throws his entire sucking mechanism out of alignment. His tongue falls into the back of his mouth, and he is unable to latch on to the breast correctly to get enough milk. Incorrect positioning of the baby at the breast can cause sore nipples and can also decrease the amount of stimulation the breasts receive. This in turn decreases the mother's milk supply. These little "archers" need to be bent into a position which allows them to latch on properly. You can nurse the baby in the classic madonna or cradle position, but his torso should be bent around your abdomen by firm pressure from your hand on his buttocks and thighs. The football hold also works well with babies who arch away from the breast. Baby is held under mother's arm on the same side he is feeding from, bent at the hips with his buttocks and legs up against the back of the chair; mother's hand has firm control of the baby's head, supporting it at the back of the neck. Bending your baby competes with and overrides his tendency to tense his muscles and arch his body.

Besides a tendency to stiffen and arch, some hypertonic babies have what is called a **tonic bite**: their lip muscles are so tight and pursed that they cannot properly latch on to the areola. This can play havoc with tender nipples. Massaging the lip muscles before a feeding will get them to relax. Pulling down your baby's lower jaw with one of your fingers during feeding will also help him latch on and nurse correctly.

Sheltered Nursing

Another problem with high need babies that affects breastfeeding is that they are hypersensitive and easily distractible. I call this kind of baby "Mr. Suck-a-Little, Look-a-Little." He goes on and off the breast several times during a feeding to have a look at all the enticing visual delights of his environment. This baby may need to be nursed in a dark quiet place, a practice called sheltered nursing.

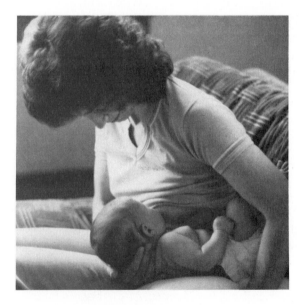

The football hold uses the back of the chair to keep baby bent at the hips during feedings.

Marathon Nursing

"The baby wants to nurse all the time, day and night," complains a tired mother. High need babies tend to go in for nursing marathons (as do all babies occasionally). They associate the breastfeeding relationship with more than just nourishment; they like the whole atmosphere of the restaurant. Marathon nursing helps them fit into their caregiving environment more comfortably. High need babies seem particularly comfortable in the nursing position and quickly learn that breastfeeding is the number one comfort measure that helps them fit into their new environment. I frequently remind parents that "babies are takers and mothers are givers." Marathon nursing asks a lot of a mother, but it is one of the most important and effective techniques for mellowing a fussy baby. Like so many other parenting investments, if you can cope with these marathon periods, every ounce of your giving will return to you when your high need baby becomes a giving child who feels right.

Improving Your Serve

Some fussy babies become very impatient if your milk is not served quickly enough. High need babies often nurse greedily, and if not immediately satisfied, they may arch back and pull away from the nipple rather than persevere until the milk flows freely. A slow milk ejection reflex (also called a let-down) may account for some feeding fussiness in these impatient babies. The following suggestions will help speed up your milk ejection reflex:

1. Create a nursing station: a calm quiet area with a comfortable chair and pillows, perhaps some pleasant music, and a table to hold snacks and drinks, diapers, burping cloths, and things to entertain an older sibling. Take the phone off the hook.

2. Take a warm shower or bath before nursing.

3. Groom and caress the baby before nursing.

4. Think your milk in. Imagine your body at work producing milk, like a flowing fountain or stream.

5. Position baby properly.

6. Massage your breasts before nursing or use a pump or manual expression to get the milk flowing before the baby latches on.

Another helpful technique for handling fussy feeders is to switch the baby to the other breast as soon as he begins to fuss. As the baby nurses on the first breast, the milk ejection reflex is beginning in the second breast. When baby is switched to the second breast, he gets more milk more quickly, a real plus for the impatient feeder.

Formula Feeding the Fussy Baby

"We've tried so hard to find the right formula," complained a frantic couple as they ran down their checklist of everything they'd tried to calm their fussy baby. In my experience, formula changes are way down on the list of things that work for colicky babies. Just to do *something*, parents may go from doctor to doctor, each of whom will suggest one formula after another. By the time the parents have tried all the formulas available on the supermarket shelf, the baby outgrows the colic, but the doctor who made the last suggestion gets credit for finally having found the right formula. Some colicky babies are helped by a change from cow's milk formula to one made with soy, although some babies who are truly allergic to cow's milk formulas will also be allergic to soy formulas. In my practice I have had many non-breastfed babies whose colic has been considerably alleviated by using a predigested formula. In these preparations, the proteins have been broken down to a less allergenic form that is easier for the infant to digest. One drawback is that they are very expensive; they cost around eight dollars a day to use. A truly colicky baby is such a drain on the family's energy that most families are willing to pay the price as a trade-off for a little more rest. I caution parents not to use soy or predigested formulas without their doctor's advice. Some babies who cannot tolerate cow's milk or soy-based formulas do well on goat's milk. Several mothers have reported that their babies seemed more comfortable when the milk or formula was warmed to body temperature.

Tips for Feeding Your Fussy Baby

Minimizing Air Swallowing

If you have a colicky baby, you need to minimize the amount of air the baby swallows while feeding. A baby is able to form a better seal with flesh on flesh then with flesh on rubber, so theoretically, babies should swallow less air while breast-feeding than while bottle-feeding.

Breastfeeding the gulper.   There are some circumstances in which breastfeeding babies gulp too much air. Engorged, distended breasts prevent baby from forming a good seal on the areola. Engorgement flattens out the nipple and areola (the pigmented area around the nipple) and makes it difficult for the baby to latch on. Consequently the baby sucks only on the nipple instead of getting part or all of the areola into his mouth. He doesn't get enough milk this way, but he does swallow a lot of air. When he cries and protests about his difficulties, he may swallow even more air. You can minimize problems with engorgement right from the start by not limiting your baby's access to the breast. Encourage him to nurse frequently and long enough to empty the breasts. Warm compresses and manual expression will release some milk before feedings, softening the areola and making it easier for baby to nurse correctly.

A strong milk ejection reflex can cause a baby to gulp air. When the milk gushes out too fast at the beginning of the feeding, the baby is overwhelmed and swallows air along with milk as he attempts to keep up with the sudden oversupply. Manually expressing a little milk prior to feeding can decrease the force of the let-down and make it easier for the baby to nurse.

Taming the barracuda.   "Barracuda" nursers like their milk fast and heavy. Some babies empty the breasts very quickly but swallow a lot of air as they continue to suck. The **burp and switch** technique minimizes air swallowing in these babies and also activates the milk ejection reflex more frequently: Nurse the baby on the first breast until he starts to slow down a bit and his eyes begin to close. Gently remove him from the breast, burp him a while, and then nurse him on the second breast until his sucking again slows down. Burp him again and go back to the first breast. About five minutes on each breast usually works best, but watch your baby's own unique signals. In this pattern the baby may nurse at each breast two or three times during a feeding, but because of the frequent switching from side to side, he never sucks on an empty breast and consequently swallows less air. After the last switch, let him suck until he is satisfied; by this time his sucking will be less greedy and he won't be swallowing as much air. This technique is also helpful for babies who are slow gainers. The burp and switch technique rewards baby with more of the satisfying, creamier hindmilk.

Feeding and burping positions.   Fussy feeders tend to spit up frequently; regurgitation is one of the calling cards of a colicky baby, whether breast- or bottle-fed. Air swallowers spit up because a trapped bubble of air settles underneath food in the stomach. When the stomach contracts, it pushes the air against the food, and like a pneumatic pump, the air forcefully expels whatever is in the way.

If you have a colicky baby, be prepared to go through many shoulder burp rags during the first six months. Regurgitation subsides markedly when baby begins to spend most of his day in the upright position. The amount the baby spits up always seems like more than it really is. If your baby is gaining weight, growing in height, and generally thriving, spitting up is most likely a temporary nuisance rather than a sign of an underlying medical problem. Babies who swallow a lot of air also tend to be frequent feeders. Once the swallowed air is removed, the stomach feels empty and signals the need for another feeding.

The art of feeding the colicky baby lies in allowing the least air to get in and getting the most air back up. Success at "winding" the baby was, in grandmother's day, the badge of an experienced baby feeder. Keeping the baby upright during feeding minimizes air swallowing and makes it easier to bring up the air later. Hold the baby at a thirty degree or greater angle all during the feeding. This allows the air to settle at the top of the stomach where it can be more easily burped out before it has a chance to make its way down through the intestines and cause colic pains. Following the feeding, keep baby upright at a ninety-degree angle for at least twenty minutes. You can sit him on your lap, drape him over your shoulder in a rocking chair, or stand up and sway back and forth rhythmically. Avoid jostling the baby after feeding or you're liable to be punished with a shot of partially digested food all over your shirt. When laying the baby down, put him on his right side and elevate the head of the

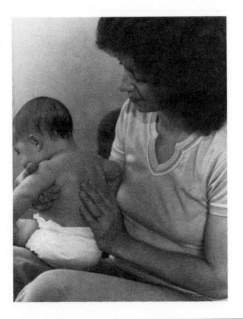

Sitting your baby upright on your knee and gently patting his back is the most effective way to bring up an air bubble.

crib slightly, approximately thirty degrees. The baby's stomach is on his left side, so this right-sided position allows the air to rise to the top of the stomach and be burped out rather than forced down into the intestines. The most effective burping position is one where baby is sitting upright on your knee or lap, slightly bent forward against your hand placed on the middle of his abdomen. Gently pat his back with your other hand. Some babies are difficult to burp, and some babies seldom need to be burped. If you don't hear a burp within ten minutes, further efforts to get out that elusive trapped air bubble will probably go unrewarded.

Overeating and the Fussy Baby
Some high need babies overeat but don't "overgrow," others overeat and "overgrow." This may be another reason for the importance of breastfeeding. Early on, high need babies associate feeding with comfort, and this is why they tend to feed often and for long stretches at a time. This is where there is an exciting difference between breastfeeding and bottlefeeding. The frequent breastfeeder does not always get the

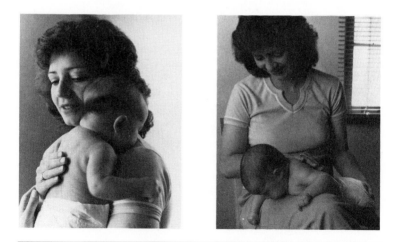

You can also burp your baby by draping him
over your lap or shoulder.

same kind of milk. When he nurses just a little bit for comfort or as a "pick-me-up" during a stressful time, he receives the lower calorie foremilk. When he nurses for a longer time to satisfy his hunger he also gets the creamier, high-calorie hindmilk. A bottle-fed baby, on the other hand, gets the same high calorie formula whether he nurses for hunger or for comfort. If bottle-fed babies fed as often as breastfed babies do, they would all be little blimps. This need for frequent feedings may explain the tendency to introduce solids earlier in bottle-fed fussy babies. Bottle-feeding mothers are required to come up with creative ways to comfort their babies since they cannot feed them as often as breastfeeding mothers.

The baby's body type has a lot to do with his growth, especially if he is a frequent feeder. High need babies with an ectomorph body type (slender and bony) may eat incessantly but yet burn off a lot of energy and remain lean. Infants with mesomorph or endomorph body types (short with pudgy hands and feet and squat large bones) are the ones who grow plump when they overeat.

Starting Solid Foods in the Fussy Baby

"It's about time you fed that baby something," said the well-meaning grandmother to her daughter who sat breastfeeding her baby for the third time in the last three hours; the obviously well nourished infant was already at the top of her class on the growth chart. Introducing solid foods has long been touted as a panacea for whatever ails the tiny baby. The generation of parents who bottle-fed their infants has not completely come to grips with the biologic fact that their grandchildren can grow quite well on nothing but their mothers' milk for the better part of the first year. Introducing solid foods too early (at three to four months) may aggravate colic; at best it has little effect on babies' behavior and seldom helps them sleep through the night. Since colicky babies have a slightly increased risk of developing allergies, I advise parents to wait with solid foods until the baby's development shows readiness rather than going by the calendar. Signs that the baby is ready for solid foods include:

> Baby sits well without support.
> Baby can pick up small objects with his thumb and forefinger.
> Baby has been marathon nursing for more than a week, but still doesn't seem satisfied.

The presence or absence of teeth doesn't affect your baby's readiness or ability to handle solid food. His grabbing at your food does not necessarily mean he's ready for solids either; at this age, he will be grabbing for everything in sight, especially anything that mother seems to be interested in.

A mashed-up very ripe banana is a good starting food because its sweet taste is very similar to mother's milk. Place a small amount of banana on the tip of your baby's tongue as a test. If the banana goes in, he's ready; if the banana comes right back at you, he's not ready. Unfortunately the most popular first foods for babies, rice cereal and bananas, are also constipating. The last thing a colicky baby needs is constipation. If you notice that your baby's stools are getting harder after starting solid foods, back off before he gets plugged up. Colicky babies who are allergic to cow's milk also have a higher incidence of being allergic to other foods such as citrus, tomatoes, and berries. It would be wise to introduce new solid foods very gradually in these babies.

Introducing solid foods too early may be particularly detrimental to high need babies. When solid foods are used as a substitute for rather than a complement to breastfeedings, the frequency of feedings decreases. The mother's milk supply diminishes, and baby may find breastfeeding less satisfying and less comforting. The baby who becomes fussier following the early introduction of solid foods may be expressing his unhappiness about decreased chances to breastfeed and his mother's low milk supply. Besides causing fussiness, introducing solid foods too early may reduce mother's coping ability. Frequent nursing keeps a mother's prolactin levels high. Babies nurse less frequently when solids are introduced (Quandt 1984). Both members of the nursing pair lose by too early an introduction to solid foods.

Junk Foods and Fussy Babies

Highly sugared foods and those with artificial colors and flavors should be avoided in all babies, but particularly in fussy babies. High need babies often grow up to be high need children, and high need children seem to be particularly vulnerable to behavioral changes caused by junk food. Inevitably, children encounter junk food in social situations in this fast food society, but if they are not given junk food during the first few years, they become more aware of its effects. They are more likely to realize that they don't feel right and don't act right after eating junk food. This is a sort of reverse addiction. When a baby grows up learning to feel right after feedings, he won't like the feeling he gets after eating junk food as an older child. He'll be more likely to turn down junk food.

Weaning the High Need Baby

"What! You're still nursing," said the shocked grandmother to her daughter who was breastfeeding her two-year-old high need baby. These babies not only have a high level of need, but the needs also last longer.

Tired mothers may ask, "How long?" I have a little sign in my office which says, "Early weaning not recommended for babies." I'd like to add here, "Especially not for high need babies." The timing of weaning is critical, and understanding the real meaning of the term weaning will help you decide when and how you should wean your high need child.

In ancient writings, weaning meant "to ripen." The word used when a fruit was ripe and ready to be picked from the vine was the same as the word used for weaning. Weaning was a positive step and wasn't associated with the end of a relationship. When a child was weaned all the people of the tribe got together and celebrated, but not because the mother was finally free of the child. Weaning was a festive occasion because the child was now ripe and ready to take on new relationships such as the beginning of formal instruction by his father and the wise men in the town. A child was weaned from the security of his mother into the arms of the culture with no break in the action. (See for example Genesis 21:8, I Samuel 1:21-24.) The image of a weaned child was used to describe a state of peace and tranquility in Psalm 131:

> I have stilled and quieted my soul,
> Like a weaned child with its mother,
> Like a weaned child is my soul within me.

Think of weaning as a time of fulfillment when the child feels so right and so ready that he looks up and says, "Thanks, Mom and Dad. I am filled with this relationship, and I am ready to take on another." Life is a series of weanings for a child: weaning from the womb, weaning from the breast, weaning from the parents' bed, weaning from home to school, from school to work. The age at which a child is ready to wean varies tremendously, especially among high need children. A child who is weaned from any of these stages before he is ready is at high risk of developing what I call diseases of premature weaning: anger, aggression, mood swings, just plain not feeling right. Too early weaning is one of the common causes of delayed fussiness. A mother might say, "She was such an easy baby for the first eight months, and now she's a bear." Tantrum-like behavior is especially common after abrupt weaning.

When I want to know the hows and whys of a certain aspect of child development, I sit back and watch what a child does over time when parents guide and channel his behavior without frustrating it. Looking back over the high need breastfed babies I have watched grow and develop, I would say that babies who are allowed unlimited access to mother usually wean sometime toward the end of the second year or later. Nap-time and bedtime nursings are usually the last ones to be given up. As a firm believer that babies do what they are designed to do, I would advise that mothers of high need babies consider the duration of breastfeeding in terms of years and not months. Weaning should take place when both members of the nursing couple are willing and able to move on.

Remember that weaning means graduating from one stage of development to another. Keep in mind that in the continuum of parenting, high need babies become high need children. As children get older their needs don't decrease; they only change. When a child is weaned from the mother's breast, the parents' roles as creative designers of a child's environment become more important. High need children are prone to becoming bored unless stimulated by an enriched environment that channels their minds into meaningful activities. Following weaning, be prepared for your high need child to up the ante continually in the parenting game.

Be prepared to get a lot of flack about nursing your toddler. Well-meaning friends and relatives are going to give you many "You're making him too dependent" messages. This is a carry-over from the days when the effectiveness of a mother was judged by how soon baby was eating three square meals a day, was sleeping through the night, and was completely weaned and toilet trained. Early independence was the goal. In my opinion, this is absolute nonsense. A baby, especially a high need baby, must go through a normal period of dependence before he can comfortably handle independence. He must be emotionally filled before he can learn how to give; he must learn how to handle attachment before he can manage detachment. I want to leave mothers of those babies who seemed destined to wean late with an encouraging thought: the most secure and independent children in my practice are those who have not been weaned before they were ready. Attend meetings of your local La Leche League group if you feel you need support for nursing your toddler in the face of criticism from friends and relatives.

Reference

Quandt, S. A. 1984. The effect of beikost on the diet of breastfed infants. *J Am Diet Assoc* 84:47.

CHAPTER 8

Fathering the Fussy Baby

"I could not have done it without my husband," confided a mother after surviving the first year of parenting her high need baby. In looking over the records of high need babies in my practice who have had a good outcome, one parenting style stands out above all the others: **a consistently involved and supportive father**.

This chapter explores many of the common feelings that fathers of fussy babies have shared with me. It will also help fathers understand why mothers of high need babies act the way they do as well as suggest ways in which fathers can make wise investments that can change fussy liabilities into creative assets.

Father Feelings and the Fussy Baby

> "All she does is nurse."
> "She's too attached."
> "We've got to get away together. I have needs, too."
> "She prefers to be with our baby rather than me."
> "The baby just won't settle down for me. I feel
>   helpless."
> "We haven't made love for weeks."

These are real feelings from real fathers who sincerely love their wives and children. But they feel frustrated with their own inability to comfort their fussy babies, and they are confused about their wives' strong attachment to their babies.

Understanding and coping with these normal feelings requires an understanding of some basic concepts, especially the concept of levels of need. Your baby comes wired with a certain level of needs, and if these needs are filled, the baby fits well into his environment. This good fit has a positive effect on his temperament, and he feels right and brings joy to his parents. If the baby's needs are not filled, his temperament may be negatively affected because he feels that he does not fit into his environment. He is at high risk for not feeling right within himself and could become a trial to his parents. In other words, babies are born to take, and somebody has to give. Who's going to be the giver? Naturally the job of filling the needs of these high need babies falls primarily on mother. I say naturally for two reasons:

1. The baby is more accustomed to the mother. After all, they have grown together for the last nine months.

2. The mother is biologically and hormonally programmed to be sensitive to the needs of her baby, especially in the first two to three years.

This does not mean that fathers have nothing to do with baby care. But it just does not come as naturally for most fathers as it does for mothers. We have to work at it harder.

Babies have a way of extracting from their mothers the amount of energy required for filling their needs and helping them fit into their new environment. Mothers, in turn, are programmed to be giving and nurturing and to supply the energy demanded by the baby. This is nature's law of supply and demand that ensures the survival of the young of the species. The mother is programmed to fill her baby's needs. But who fills the mother's needs? Father has to supply this missing ingredient.

In order for the parenting economic system to work, there are certain conditions that have to be met. These conditions prepare the mother for her job and help her grow and mature. They build up her stamina, her milk supply, her levels of mothering hormones, and her overall sensitivity to her baby. She not only can survive, but also thrive as the mother of a high need baby. These conditions include:

A positive birthing experience.
Continued mother-baby togetherness in the postpartum period.
Unrestricted breastfeeding.
Mother and baby sleeping close to each other, that is, sharing sleep.
Responding promptly to baby's cries.
Not weaning until the baby is ready.

These mothering practices are a bit demanding, but most, if not all of them, are necessary if you have a high need baby. They really do build up a mother's ability to cope.

A new mother cannot be all things to all people. If she is blessed with a high need baby, she has to reapportion her energies. The time and caring which were previously parcelled out in appropriate amounts to the people around her are now directed primarily toward the baby. Other people feel left out, including her husband. During that short period of time when the baby is so totally dependent on the mother, this redirection of time, emotion, and energy is very necessary.

Sexual Feelings

Fathers of high need babies also feel confused at their wives' apparent lack of sexual interest. An understanding of the hormonal changes that go on in your wife after birth may help you to understand this temporary lack of sexual drive. Before the baby is born, a woman's sexual hormones have a greater effect on her behavior than her maternal hormones. After giving birth this changes, and the mothering hormones predominate. Providing the environment is supportive and the mother is willing and able, the mothering hormones will dominate the sexual hormones as long as this is necessary to fill the baby's needs. This doesn't mean that your wife has lost interest in you sexually; it just means that the energies which were previously directed toward you are temporarily redirected toward your baby. This is how the system was designed to function, especially with a high need baby.

Everyone makes demands of the new mother, especially the baby. By evening time, it is very normal for a mother to feel, "Don't bother me. Just let me go to sleep." Overwhelmed by physical closeness to the baby and perhaps by the demands of another small child, mothers of high need babies often tell me, "I feel all touched out."

Help at Home

Provide your wife with some domestic help to free her from commitments which drain her energy away from the baby. Help with the housework yourself, or if you can afford it, consider hiring someone to clean or do whatever needs to be done. In my experience, mothers of high need babies don't get worn out so much by the baby alone. It's all the additional commitments that really do them in. Avoid putting pressure on your wife to be the perfect hostess, social chairman, entertainer, and housekeeper. This is also a time to accept the fact that your castle may never again be as tidy as it once was. Freeing a mother from other responsibilities is especially important when the baby is going through a particularly demanding period. If your baby is in one of those "all he wants to do is nurse" periods, be sure all mother *has* to do is nurse. Even though we as fathers cannot breastfeed our babies, we can create an environment that helps our wives nurse better.

Respect the Mother's Sensitivity to the Baby's Cries

Avoid offering the "let the baby cry it out" advice. Keep in mind that mothers are wired differently than fathers in regard to sensitivity to a baby's cries. A baby's cry sets up a physiologic change in the mother, but father experiences no such change. When and how to respond to a baby's cries is one case where mother certainly knows best.

Avoid Pressuring the New Mother

I've spent many hours counseling young mothers who feel that their husbands are putting pressure upon them to go against their mothering instincts. These husbands are causing their wives to feel guilty about not being perfect, submissive wives. The most common expression of this kind of pressure is the "we need to get away" syndrome. Let me share with you a real situation which illustrates this point.

Dan and Susan were proud parents of a three-month-old high need baby girl, Jessica. Susan was doing well at meeting Jessica's needs and having some energy left over for herself and her relationship with her husband. Both Jessica and Susan were thriving, but Dan was feeling left out. Dan had a chance to close a big business deal across the country and figured it was time that he and Susan got away together alone. He pressured Susan to leave Jessica behind (and wean her, too) so that the two of them could fly away and rekindle their romance. Dan also felt that Susan would be an asset in closing the deal.

In talking to both of them, I convinced Dan that he was putting Susan in a no-win situation. One side of her felt that yes, she would like to get away with Dan, but her deep maternal instincts told her that Jessica was not ready to be left alone. If they did leave her behind, the whole family would lose: Susan would not be the relaxed and romantic mate that Dan wanted with him on his trip, and Jessica would make them pay for this premature weaning when they got back.

The solution? Dan, Susan, and Jessica took off together for New York. (Jessica nursed all the way from coast to coast.) They were surprised to discover that Dan's business contact also had his wife and baby along. The wife exclaimed, "I'm so happy you brought your baby along, too. We have one of those babies who just can't be left." The two fathers had an instant rapport because they had both bucked the same system and shown that their babies had top priority in their lives. The business deal was closed successfully.

I hope this explanation of normal maternal feelings will help fathers cope with their own feelings. You have not been displaced by your baby, but the energies which were previously directed toward you are now redirected toward your baby. This is a season of the marriage, a time to mother, a

The time when babies are small and demand large amounts of energy is only one of many seasons of marriage.

time to father. If you nurture your wife as she nurtures your baby, her energies will return to you and at such a high level of warmth and maturity that you will know that you have made a good investment.

The Care and Feeding of New Mothers

A new mother needs mothering, too. The most important ingredient in parenting the high need baby—more important than breastfeeding, sleeping with the baby, responding to his cries— is a **stable and fulfilling marriage**. In order for the attachment style of parenting to work, it needs to be performed under the umbrella of the father loving and nurturing the mother as she nurtures their child. At this point you may be thinking, "I understand the system, but what can I do to help?" One father of a high need newborn put it very well: "I can't always console our baby, but I can do everything possible to make it easier for my wife to console him."

Be Involved Early

Ideally a father's involvement with parenting begins during pregnancy. Attend prepared childbirth classes with your wife so that you can be present and involved in the birth of your baby. After the baby is born, pitch in and help: change diapers, bathe the baby, wash dishes, cook, clean house, anything that can free up your wife to do what no one else can do—be a mother to your child. Some fathers may feel that domestic chores are not their job, but mother's and father's roles are not so clearly defined as they were years ago. Back then a new mother was likely to be surrounded with an extended family which pitched in and took over domestic chores in the first weeks after the birth of a baby. Many young families today do not enjoy the luxury of living close to their extended families. In today's mobile society, father's role in the family needs to be extended.

Communicate Your Commitment

Sit down with your wife regularly and reaffirm your commitment to her as a husband and to your baby as a father. You might even read this chapter and discuss it together. In our family we have a custom that I call "inventory time." From

---

Drifting Apart

Mary and Tom came into my office one day with anxious looks on their faces. Divorce seemed imminent. Mary related that she had been saddled with a high need baby. She tried so hard to be a "good" mother: she took her baby with her everywhere, nursed on demand, slept with the baby, picked him up every time he cried, and was always at baby John's beck and call. Because Tom didn't know much about babies and crying babies scared him, Mary seldom released the baby into his care. This only reinforced Tom's feeling of inadequacy, and he sought consolation in longer hours at the office. As Mary got more and more into her mothering, Tom got more and more into his job; the two drifted farther and farther apart, and baby John kept fussing. Mary increased her attachment mothering, while Tom began forming some outside "attachments" of his own. Mary realized that she and Tom were not communicating but justified it by thinking, "My baby needs me. Tom is a big boy. He can take care of himself." Fortunately this couple had the wisdom to realize that they were headed down the wrong road. They sought help and the situation had a happy ending.

I include this real life story in order to urge couples to realize that healthy family dynamics must have a balance. Mutual sensitivity keeps a two parent family thriving and intact. This is vitally important in the parenting of a high need child. I feel very strongly that a good marriage is necessary for parenting the high need baby. Unfortunately, when mothers and fathers are not working together in parenting their high need child, the marriage undergoes a lot of stress and strain.

time to time I sit down with my wife and simply ask her how she's doing. You may be surprised when she breaks down and confides, "I thought you'd never ask. I'm getting so burned out." Periodic "I care" messages give your wife the security that you are commited to this entire relationship. Impress upon her that you truly understand the concept of the high need baby and reassure her that you are all in this together.

Tune In

A mother who was under a lot of stress because of the demands of her high need baby once told me, "I'd have to hit my husband over the head before he'd realize that I'm giving out." Dads, while mothers are noted for their untiring energy in giving, they don't always know when their energy is giving out. They will continue to run a long time on an almost empty tank without calling for help. Be sensitive to the early warning signals of maternal burnout and come to the rescue early.

Gentling Tips for Fathers

It is very frustrating for dads when their babies don't respond to their comforting measures. Babies do have a preference for mother, but there are things that dads can do sometimes even better than mothers. See Chapter Five for more about gentling techniques such as warm fuzzies, freeway fathering, and colic dances. Here are some more tips especially for fathers on comforting fussy babies.

Sing to Your Baby

While it is true that most babies pay closer attention to the higher pitch of mother's voice, some babies are soothed more easily by low-pitched male voices. Sing humming, droning, rather monotonous songs such as "Old Man River."

Take Over during High Need Times

Babies don't time their fussy periods conveniently. They seem to fuss most in the late afternoon or early evening—a time which unfortunately coincides with father coming home. Fussy babies have better periods and worse periods during the day. Unfortunately dads usually see more of the worse periods. This does absolutely nothing for the father-child relationship. More often it prompts the question "Is he always like this?"

You can really make points with your tired wife by taking over during the fussy part of the day. This is the scenario: Tired dad arrives home and is greeted by a tired mom and a fussy baby. Instead of sitting down to relax and unwind from the day's tensions undisturbed, tired dad scoops up the fussy baby and waltzes him off for a car ride, a long walk, or maybe just a dance around the house, leaving the tired wife with the message, "You do something just for yourself." Try this, dads. You may surprise your wife so much that she may have a surprise or two in store for you when you return.

Mothers can help avoid some of this late afternoon fussing by putting babies down for naps later in the afternoon. Baby then awakens shortly before dad arrives home, and he at least is not greeted by a tired baby. This generally is a lot easier on the whole family than keeping the baby up in hopes that he'll fall asleep early in the evening and the adults can finally have some peace and quiet together.

What's in It for You?

Dads, if you have been consistently involved in fathering your high need baby and in nurturing your wife, you will profit. First of all, you will know your child better. By spending more time with your child, especially during those high need periods, you will begin to see not only the difficult side of your child's temperament but also its strong points. There really are many.

You will also feel more adept as a father. Many fathers are unjustly portrayed as bumbling males who stick their fingers with diaper pins. This simply is not true. There is such a thing as father's intuition, but we males have to work at it harder. It takes longer to develop than mothers' intuition.

Increasing your involvement with your high need baby will also help your marriage prosper. One of the greatest ways that you can increase the respect your wife has for you is to care for her child. Your high need child will bring out the best in you.

CHAPTER 9

Nighttime Parenting of the High Need Child

"Why do high need babies need more of everything but sleep?" asked a tired mother. One of the "for better or for worse" aspects of nighttime parenting is that babies usually carry their daytime temperament into the night.

Some studies have shown that so-called easy babies go to sleep easier and stay asleep longer than difficult babies (Sears 1985; Weissbluth and Liel 1983). In these studies, babies with more sensitive temperaments slept an average of two hours less at night and one hour less during the day. This is a paradox for tired parents. You would think that high need babies would need more sleep; their parents do. One father aptly put it this way: "When it comes to sleep, I'm a high need parent."

Why High Need Babies Sleep Differently

High need babies carry the temperamental traits of their waking personalities into the nighttime. Parents will often describe their special baby as "tiring but bright." This brightness is what keeps high need babies awake. They seem to be constantly awake and aware. It's as if they were endowed with an internal light that is not easily turned off.

The Stimulus Barrier

Babies have a **stimulus barrier** which enables them to block out unpleasant stimuli. One of the ways that most babies block out environmental stimuli is by falling asleep. High need babies have an immature stimulus barrier. Their sensory thresholds are lower; in other words you do not have to bother them much in order to get a reaction. Hunger, discomfort, cold, and loneliness tend to awaken a high need baby easily, even though a baby with a higher sensory threshold may sleep through these same disturbances. Part of high need babies' increased sensitivity comes from being constantly aware of their environment. They are always tuned into and processing the delights of the world around them. Their radar systems don't shut down easily.

Sleep Maturity

Another reason why high need babies sleep less is that they take longer to develop sleep maturity. There are two general stages of sleep: light sleep and deep sleep. It is much easier to arouse an individual from light sleep than from deep sleep. Babies have a greater percentage of light sleep than adults do; this difference has both survival and developmental benefits. As a baby grows older the amount of light sleep diminishes and the amount of deep sleep increases. Babies begin to sleep better.

High need babies take longer to develop sleep maturity. They seem to have longer and more frequent periods of light sleep. Consequently they are restless and squirming during a large part of the night. (I suspect that these babies also enjoy a more intense kind of deep sleep; they really seem "zonked" when they are in the deep sleep stage.) Periods of light sleep alternate with periods of deep sleep throughout the night. As babies move from one sleep state to the next they go through a period in which they are vulnerable to waking. High need babies seem to have more of these vulnerable periods and therefore are prone to waking up more frequently.

Sleep Survival Tips

Nursing Down

It is totally unrealistic for parents of a high need baby to put him down in a crib and expect to watch him settle himself into a deep slumber. It seldom works that way. These babies need to be parented to sleep rather than just put to bed. They need help shutting down. A technique that has been successful in our family is what we call **nursing down**: rock your baby, walk with him, and nurse him as a before-bed ritual. What you are actually doing is gentling your baby into tuning out the distractions of his world and enticing him into the initial period of light sleep. You then continue nursing and rocking your baby in your arms until he appears to have drifted through the initial period of light sleep (approximately twenty minutes). He now enters the deep sleep state and will seem to melt into your arms. Now you can put him down. If you try to put him down from your arms into bed too early, before he is fully into the deep sleep phase, he very likely will wake up and demand that you repeat the whole bedtime ritual. In fact, it probably will take longer the second time around. These babies are so ultrasensitive that a change of position or the change of gravity that comes with going from your arms down onto the bed is enough to awaken them from light sleep. Experienced mothers frequently say, "The baby has to be fully asleep before I can put him down."

Nestle Nursing
In some ultrasensitive babies this rock and nurse ritual is
not enough. They settle better if after the nursing down phase
mother and baby simply curl up next to each other and nurse
off to sleep. These bright little babies do not seem to want
to change levels of consciousness (from awake to asleep)
alone and need to fall asleep surrounded by somebody.

The Advantages of Sharing Sleep
Where should the baby sleep? I usually tell parents that wherever all three of you get the most sleep is the right arrangement for your family. In my experience, most high need
babies sleep better when they sleep with their parents. (In
fact, to most high need babies, crib is a four-letter word.)
Most parents sleep better this way, too. It is the nature of
these sensitive babies to want harmony in their environment
both by day and by night. Sleeping with your baby is often
called the family bed. I prefer to call this beautiful arrangement **sharing sleep**. Babies share more than the physical
space with their parents; they also share sleep cycles.

Sharing sleep cycles.   Sharing sleep helps mother and baby
organize their sleep cycles. They sleep in harmony with each
other. Mother and baby are close to each other when baby
begins to stir as he enters a vulnerable period for night-
waking. Mother can then nurse the baby right through this
vulnerable period of lighter sleep and help him re-enter the
state of deep sleep while preventing his waking up completely. Mothers who begin this arrangement early enough
(right after birth) usually find that their own light sleep stages
coincide with their babies'. Mother's deep sleep is not inter-
rupted, and she feels more rested.

Easier breastfeeding.   With the sharing sleep arrangement
it is not necessary for the baby to wake up crying in order
to signal feeding time. If the baby wakes up hungry and alone,
he must cry to summon his mother. If mother is not close
by, he must cry even harder. By the time mother arrives both

she and baby are fully awake, and it takes longer for both of them to get back to sleep after the feeding. In this instance, baby learns to cry harder; this works against your efforts to mellow your high need baby's temperament and teach him to cry better rather than harder. Mothers who sleep with their babies may have higher prolactin levels, and thus they get an added hormonal boost for surviving and thriving with their high need babies. Babies who sleep with their mothers are also less likely to wean before they are ready.

Over the past ten years I have advocated the sharing sleep arrangement in my pediatric practice and enjoyed it in our own family. It is beautiful and it works! In general, I have noticed that babies who share sleep with their parents exude a feeling of rightness and security—the serenity of a child who is in harmony with his world by day and by night.

Benefits of Bedtime Rituals

Parenting a child to sleep instead of simply putting him to bed has a mellowing effect on his daytime behavior. The state of relaxation immediately before drifting off to sleep is called the alpha state. It is believed that thoughts which occur during the alpha state are the thoughts most likely to be remembered and carried over into awakening in the morning. If a child goes off to sleep at mother's breast or in father's arms, he feels right. A child who goes to sleep feeling right is more likely to awake feeling right and will begin the next day on a positive note.

Contrast the child who is put down in a crib and left to cry himself to sleep alone. He goes to bed angrily and is therefore likely to awaken in an angry mood. He certainly is destined to "get up on the wrong side of the bed." A little extra energy spent with your child at the end of the day may save you a lot of wasted energy the next day.

Bedtime is also a prime time for planting behavior-mellowing ideas in a child's mind. One creative father of a high need two-year-old was desperate to calm down his overactive son. He made a tape of soothing environmental sounds: a babbling brook, waves on the beach, flute and harp music in the background, and the soft voice of father narrating a fairy tale that portrayed nice animals in the forest who did nice things for each other all day long. This father's child went to sleep calmly and awoke calmly.

Parents may also use the parenting-to-bed ritual to plant ethical thoughts in a child's mind. This is best accomplished for a toddler by narrating simple fairy tales which contain moral lessons. Older children enjoy just lying in bed and talking with a parent. A lot will be said then that otherwise might be lost.

References

Sears, W. 1985. *Nighttime Parenting*. Franklin Park, Il.: La Leche League International.

Weissbluth, M. and Liel, K. 1983. Sleep patterns, attention span and infant temperament. *J Dev Behav Pediatr* 4:34.

CHAPTER 10

How to Avoid Burnout in the Mothering Profession

"I can't handle this any longer. I'm not enjoying motherhood. I can't cope, but I have to." These are real feelings shared by caring mothers who are exhausted and approaching the point of burnout.

What is burnout? Every profession demands a certain level of energy from its practitioners. When the demands of a profession exceed an individual's available energy, that person begins to "burn out" and can no longer adequately function within his or her profession. Burnout in the mothering profession means that for a variety of reasons, the demands for your energy exceed your supply. Your ability to cope wears thinner and thinner, and the small amount of energy you have left dwindles to a bare minimum. In short, you are surviving but not thriving. Parenting the high need child and the lack of sleep that goes with the job are frequent causes of parent burnout.

The main goal of the attachment style of parenting is that you enjoy your child. Burnout keeps you from reaching this goal. Understanding the causes of maternal burnout can help you recognize its warning signs as well as take preventive measures to avoid it.

Causes of Burnout

Perhaps the number one reason why burnout is so common is the Supermom myth. Never before have mothers been required or expected to do so much for so many with so little support. In those critical few months after birth, many mothers are not permitted the luxury of being just a mother. In fact, the culture relays the subtle message that "only mothering" is a bit demeaning for the modern woman who has so many options. Shortly after birth, many mothers are expected to resume their previous roles as loving and giving wives, gourmet cooks, keepers of immaculate houses, gracious hostesses, and contributors to the family income. The baby meanwhile is expected to fit conveniently into this lifestyle. "Life in the fast lane" and motherhood are often incompatible, even with modern labor-saving devices.

What is even more exhausting to the new mother is that she often enters motherhood with no real role models to follow and without an extended family to turn to for immediate advice and help. Today's mother is alone. All those convenient appliances make poor company, and they have nothing to teach a new mother about babies or about parenting. Many women enter the mothering profession with inadequate preparation, unrealistic expectations, and a lack of coping skills.

Babies Are Not to Blame

Along with the Supermom myth comes the erroneous assumption that the baby is always to blame for maternal burnout. In my experience, this is usually not the case. It is true
that having a high need baby contributes to exhaustion, but
I have rarely seen a case of burnout that could be attributed
solely to the baby. If you look into each situation carefully,
there is usually some other factor that drains away the
mother's energy, diverting it from what she should be doing
(or wants to be doing) to what she is required to be doing
(or thinks she is required to be doing).

The mother and baby are designed to operate as a unit.
The supply of energy needed for the mother to meet the
baby's demands will be available as long as two conditions
are met:

1. The mother is allowed and encouraged to operate
   in an environment which allows her intuitive
   mothering skills to develop (the attachment style
   of parenting).

2. Other demands do not drain away the mother's
   energy.

Burnout is more likely to occur in highly motivated mothers.
You have to be on fire before you can get burned out. Experts agree that burnout is more common in women who
strive to be the perfect mother and want to do the things
that are best for their babies (Procaccini and Kiefaber 1983).
I mention this to alleviate the fear that some mothers express: "I must not be a good mother because I have these
burned-out feelings." I have a real interest in maternal burnout because I realize that many mothers who are attracted
to the attachment style of parenting are mothers who, because they want very much to do what's best for their babies, are at risk for burnout. The attachment style of parenting
itself does not cause burnout, but practicing it in an unsup-
portive environment can raise the risk.

Mother's Stress Test

Many factors predispose mothers and fathers to burnout. These include:

1. A history of difficulty in coping with stress and a tendency toward depression as a reaction to major changes.

2. Ambivalent feelings during your pregnancy, especially about how the child will interfere with your current lifestyle.

3. High recognition in a career before becoming a mother.

4. Poor prenatal preparation and unrealistic expectations of what babies are like.

5. Lack of role models for attachment parenting; lack of a good role model in your own mother.

6. A stressful labor and delivery that did not go according to your expectations.

7. Medical problems at birth which separated mother and baby.

8. A high need baby.

9. Mismatch of temperaments between mother and baby (for example, a fussy baby and a mother with a low tolerance for fussing).

10. Marital discord and the expectation that a child will solve the problems.

11. An uninvolved father.

12. A highly motivated and compulsive mother.

13. A mother committed to too many outside activities.

14. A move or extensive remodeling or redecorating.

15. Illness in mother, father, or baby.

16. Financial pressures.

17. A barrage of conflicting baby care advice.

18. Successive babies who are close in age, that is, less than two years apart.

19. Family discord, for example, problems with older children.

Mother burnout is rarely the result of only one of these factors. It usually involves a combination of factors which have a cumulative effect. Burnout is usually a problem that involves the whole family. Rarely is it the mother's problem alone.

Recognizing the Early Warning Signs

There is a saying in medicine that the earlier an illness is recognized the milder the medicine and the more effective the treatment. In my office, I place a red star at the top of the chart of a baby whose mother exhibits a history with several of the risk factors listed above. This is to remind me that this mother is at risk for burning out and that preventive "medicine" should be administered.

The earliest warning sign (I call these signs "red flags") of impending burnout is the feeling that you are not enjoying your child. This indicates that you and your child are not in harmony with each other. Harmony between parent and child is absolutely vital to achieving the real benefit of the attachment style of parenting—enjoying your child.

Another red flag is the feeling, "I'm not a good mother." Occasional feelings of shaky confidence are normal in the mothering profession. These feelings flow naturally from a sincere love for your child. The more you care for another person, the more vulnerable you are to feeling inadequate in that relationship. But when these feelings of inadequacy persist and increase, you should seek help—before your confidence is totally shaken and alternative forms of self-fulfillment have enticed you to withdraw from your child.

Survival Tips That Will Lower Your Risk

If you have several of the above risk factors or have experienced early warning signs of burnout, you can take precautions to prevent your feelings from developing into full-scale burnout. You can lessen your chances of burning out.

Prepare Yourself

During your pregnancy, give careful consideration to how your new baby will change your lifestyle, especially if you have an exciting, prestigious career from which you receive lots of recognition. This is especially important if you have ambivalent feelings about your desire or ability to totally immerse yourself in your baby and temporarily postpone or give up your career outside the home. Join a support group in order to develop realistic expectations of what babies are like. Many new parents don't realize how time-consuming a new baby actually is; a tiny baby can completely change a predictable, organized lifestyle. "Nobody told me it would be this way" is a common statement from mothers who had unrealistic expectations of the mothering profession.

A major part of your preparation is getting your husband involved early in your pregnancy, as well as during labor, delivery, and the postpartum period. In my experience the most common cause of mother burnout is an uninvolved father.

A typical example of what happens when a high-risk mother and an uninvolved father don't communicate was shown in the movie *Kramer vs. Kramer*. Mrs. Kramer had been a career woman before the couple had their first child. Just as she had been a perfect career woman, she tried to be a perfect mother. Meanwhile Mr. Kramer became more involved in his work and less involved at home. He never really got a handle on fathering. Even when he was home, all he could talk about was the excitement at his job. He made his wife feel that he alone was doing something worthwhile. The combination of isolation, lack of recognition, and not seeing the immediate results of all her dedication soon led Mrs. Kramer to leave her family. No one, least of all her husband, recognized the signs that warned that she was burning out.

Practice the Attachment Style of Parenting

Attachment parenting helps you get in harmony with your baby. It widens your acceptance level, makes your expectations more realistic, and generally increases your confidence. Restraining your responses to your baby leads to chronic disenchantment with the whole mothering role. The attachment style of parenting gives an added boost to maternal stamina with an increase in prolactin, the perseverance hormone.

Know Your Limits

One night I was giving a talk on "immersion mothering" which involves really getting tuned into your child. After the talk, a grandmother came up to me and politely said, "Dr. Sears, do you realize that 'immersion' means getting in over your head?" Mothers who are burning out may feel as if they are in over their heads.

Mothers should not only have realistic expectations of their babies; they also need to have realistic expectations of their own tolerance level. Mothers vary greatly in their ability to cope with a high need baby. This statement is not meant to be critical of mothers. It is simply a fact. Some mothers tolerate stress better than others. Some are frazzled by one crying baby while others are not ruffled even by several babies and children crawling all over them like a human jungle gym. It is important to be honest with yourself and accept your coping abilities for what they are. Do not let yourself get into situations that require you to go beyond your personal tolerance level. For example, if your first baby is a high need baby and you do not have a high level of tolerance for fussing, it would probably be unwise to add to the strain by having another baby right away. Be wise enough to admit that in your particular situation spacing your children farther apart will lessen your risk of burning out.

"I'm Not Going to Let That Baby Run My Life"

"When I was pregnant I set down some rules that I planned to follow after our child was born. I wasn't going to let a baby manipulate me or run our lives. I wanted to get her on a schedule as soon as possible. I was determined not to be one of those mothers whose baby was hanging on her all the time.

"My labor was long and painful. The baby kept spitting up formula during the month after her birth, so I tried breastfeeding. I had been given a shot to dry up my milk so I needed to use a nursing supplementer to bring my milk back in. By eight months, I had a good milk supply, and the baby was demanding to be held and nursed all the time. I didn't want her to get into the habit of needing to be held all the time. So I weaned her cold turkey at nine months. I can't get anything done. I feel trapped but I can't resign. I have tried to let her cry it out but I can't stand to listen to her. I had no parenting models to follow. My mother spanked me whenever I got out of line. Kristine has become an intensely angry baby."

This mother is burned out. She was at high risk from early on: poor parenting models, unrealistic expectations, a traumatic birth experience, mother-baby separation after birth, an injection that suppresses the natural maternal hormones. This mother and baby never got in harmony with each other. The baby demanded the attachment style of parenting until she got it, but the mother was reluctant. The mother would have profited from a counselor who could have pointed out the mismatch between her expectations and her baby's temperament.

Some mothers feel that they are losing control of the situation when they are open to their babies. During several months of counseling in which I advised this mother to use the attachment style of parenting, I reassured her that responding to her baby would eventually pay off, but because she was playing "catch-up," it might take some time. She and her baby finally began to enjoy each other, and her closing comments were, "I wish somebody had pointed this out to me a lot earlier."

During my many years as a pediatrician and father I have been amazed at how mothers cope so well (at least on the surface) with the many stresses of child rearing and family life. But I have also observed that many women do not know and accept their own limits. This is especially true of highly motivated mothers whose desire to give of themselves often completely overpowers their ability to know when they are giving out. This may be a result, in part, of the hormonal effects of attachment parenting. Mothers vary in their ability to hear and heed their own distress signals. They also may not know how to react to these signals once they recognize them.

How Fathers Can Help Mothers Avoid Burnout

Just as mothers are not noted for their ability to recognize the signs of impending burnout, fathers also are not known for their sensitivity to their wives' distress signals. The most common cause of maternal burnout is an uninvolved father.

Fathers, be sensitive to those factors which put your wife at risk for burning out, and be alert for the early warning signs mentioned above. Don't wait for your wife to tell you that she can't cope. Wives seldom confide their ambivalent feelings to their husbands; they don't want to appear weak or risk shattering their husband's image of them as a perfect mother.

Harmony is as important in the mother-father relationship as it is in the mother-child relationship. To be sensitive to imminent burnout you have to be tuned in to the stresses in your individual family situation which compete with your wife's mothering energy. For example, as an involved father you can create an atmosphere which makes it easier for your wife to breastfeed successfully. By "mothering the mother" you can help her develop a breastfeeding relationship that, because of the hormones involved, gives her the strength and desire to mother the baby.

Father's involvement is especially important if you have been blessed with a high need child. A father who is not involved early on may never become comfortable with consoling the fussy baby, handling a temper tantrum, or disciplining an unruly child. Lack of early involvement has a snowballing effect. The less involved you are, the less comfortable you are with your effectiveness as a father. This can lead some men to withdraw from both the high need child and the family situation and retreat into interests outside the home where they feel more comfortable and competent. The combination of a high need child, a burned-out mother, and a withdrawn father can lead to the collapse of the entire family structure.

The mother of a high need child who was nearing the point of burnout recently shared an example of this kind of situation with me. She confided, "By the time my husband

---

"I'll Never Have Any More Kids"

"Jessica was so trying for so many months that I started reminding myself that I would never have to do this again if I chose not to. It relieved some of my anguish to think this. When Jessica was seven months old, I approached my husband about having a vasectomy. He thought about it and had it done. Now I deeply regret it. Had Jessica been an easier baby I never would have suggested it. But as she approaches her first birthday, I see how beautifully she is doing and how well we have done together. I wish that we had waited longer to make such an important decision. I would tell other parents not to make a decision about having more children based on the experience of living with a fussy baby. You may regret it later when the fussy baby calms down."

This is wise counsel from a grieving mother. Sterilization is a decision often based on present circumstances (which may change), worry about the future (which you can't predict), and impulsiveness. Your decision may change as you change. Having a fussy baby eventually brought out the best in these parents, but it also caused them to make a bad decision.

---

comes home I am a wreck. However, he expects our child to be bathed, in her pajamas, and ready for bed. The quicker we can get her off to bed so that we can settle down for a quiet evening with just the two of us, the more pleased he is." This is a classic situation: Mother is worn out by the end of the day, and the high need child needs some prime time with dad in the evening. Dad comes home from work to his castle and discovers that neither the queen nor the little princess are up to regal behavior. A father who has not been consistently involved with the child does not know how to handle the situation. Early evening is a particularly stressful time for many families. It is a time when mother's energy is giving out and father wants to wind down. The child, however, is winding up in anticipation of the change from day-time with mother to an evening with father. This touchy situation is further compounded by the fact that children are often the most tired and therefore the least enjoyable at that time of the day or evening when father is home with them.

The attachment style of parenting works only if child care is shared by both parents. A father who is sensitive to the risk of mother burnout will frequently administer preventive medicine: "I'll take over. You do something just for yourself." An uninvolved father recently sent his wife into my office for some counseling with the subtle message that "it must be her fault that we have a demanding kid whom she can't handle." Since father sent mother in for some treatment, I felt that it was my professional duty to prescribe the most effective medicine I knew of. I gave mother a prescription and said, "Now be sure your husband fills this for you." The prescription read, "Administer one dose of a caring husband and involved father three times a day and before bedtime until symptoms subside."

The Carry-Over Effect of Burnout
Maternal burnout often carries over into the marriage. A burned-out mother often becomes a burned-out wife. Her feelings of exhaustion and ineffectiveness often mushroom into general feelings of inadequacy as a person. Depression

sets in. She pays less attention to her own grooming and appearance. She may vent her frustrations on her husband, especially if she feels a lack of involvement and support from him. Many men tend to feel that if their wives cannot handle the situation, then they cannot handle it either. They withdraw rather than increase their involvement. Because both partners are insensitive to each other's needs, they drift apart, and the result is marriage burnout as well as maternal burnout. Quite honestly, dads, this is why involved fathering is such a good investment for you. By keeping your wife from burning out, your marriage will mature, and you yourself will ultimately profit.

Be Sensitive to Each Other

Just as fathers are often not sensitive to the early signs of maternal burnout, mothers may not confide in their husbands. They may be unwilling to release their child into their husbands' care, or they may not be assertive about their husbands playing an active role in child care. Without harmony and mutual sensitivity it is very difficult for families to survive the pressures of contemporary society. Fathers, be sensitive and anticipate the new mother's needs. Mothers, be open to your husband's suggestion that your reserves are exhausted and something has to give. Mothers can sit down and make an "I need help" list. Write down all the daily chores which compete with mothering for your energy: housework, car pools, meetings, etc. Tell your husband exactly where you need help in all of these areas and be open to his ideas, especially if he suggests that several of these seemingly important daily tasks don't have to get done.

Define Priorities

Very early in your mothering career you will realize that you cannot be all things to all people and that a list of priorities is necessary for survival. Be realistic about how much time and energy you must spend on your family situation, especially if you have a high need child or a large family with close-in-age children. Sit down and make a list of all those daily activities which drain away your energies. With the support of your husband, scratch as many of these activities off the list as possible. For example, an exhausted mother recently told me that she was a compulsive housekeeper until one day she looked at the kitchen floor and realized, "That floor doesn't have feelings. No one's life is going to be affected if that floor doesn't get scrubbed every day. My baby is a baby for a very short time, and she has feelings." This is part of maturing as a mother. You have to realize that if ten things need to be done and you only have energy for eight of them, you should only do eight things. Just be sure to include all the ones with feelings.

Do Something for Yourself

It may be unrealistic for some mothers to think that one role can satisfy all their needs for fulfillment. This is a high risk situation for burnout. An unfulfilled mother is no good to anyone, especially herself. Realistically, babies are takers and mothers are givers, and babies will continue to take until their own needs are completely filled. Babies are designed this way so that they can grow up to be loving, giving adults. But a mother cannot give continuously without being recharged periodically. Most mothers, especially those with high need children, need to discipline themselves to take some time to do things they want to do—not just things they have to do. Dedicated mothers of high need children are not always able to admit that they need time off, especially if they are isolated in a situation in which taking time off seems impossible. Oftentimes it is necessary for a sensitive and caring husband, a friend, or a health care professional to step in and **release** the mother for a bit of time off. As one mother told me, "I just needed someone to give me permission to take some time for me. I felt that my child needed me constantly." Intervention like this is aimed at helping mother and father nurture themselves in order that they can better nurture their children. This is not meant to encourage a mother to become selfish or uncaring about her child but rather to help her develop staying power in order that she can continue to mother in the way the child was designed to be mothered.

One of my patients who had been a concert pianist prior to having her first baby provides a good example of a mother taking time for herself. She was blessed with a high need baby and had made a commitment to mothering, so she devoted her full time and energy to her baby. She also received help from a highly involved father and supportive friends. Her baby was the type of high need baby who demanded mother's full energy twenty-four hours a day. Nevertheless, this mother had the wisdom to take a half-hour each day to sit down at her piano and enjoy her skill. Her child would fuss while she played, but she had decided that this was her time and she deserved it. She did not leave her child alone; he was allowed to play with his toys in the same room. After a while the child began to respect mother's private time, as if he sensed that she felt better afterwards and that he benefited in the long run.

In another family situation, the mother refused to take any time off, but the father had the wisdom and insight to recognize early signs of burnout. Twice a week he came home early from work and insisted that his wife go down to the health spa and relax. Two things helped this mother to accept the idea: She trusted her husband's wisdom and judgment (an example of family harmony), and she felt comfortable leaving the baby in the husband's arms since he had been involved in the baby's care from early on. Even in societies where babies are almost constantly in arms, they are often in the arms of family members other than the mother.

Another mother put it this way: "I feel that even after birth my labor never really stopped and that I'm still pregnant with a two-year-old. My life is a circle that revolves around her. What I need is a square which encloses her circle but leaves some corners just for me."

Nighttime Parenting and Family Burnout

Children's sleep difficulties can place great stress on a family and contribute to child abuse and broken marriages. Your child's sleep problem becomes a family problem when his frequent night-waking exceeds your ability to cope. What happens when you have reviewed all the possible causes of night-waking and tried all the tips for inducing sleep and nothing works? Occasionally I talk to a mother who is trying to be a perfect nighttime parent but as a result is so exhausted that her effectiveness during the day as a mother, wife, and person is greatly diminished. There simply is not enough energy to go around if the mother is up with the child all night and is expected to meet everyone's needs during the day. I find this a most difficult situation in which to counsel parents, and I usually start by saying, "You have a problem and you're not going to like any of the solutions for it, but we must admit that you have to do something. Something has to go. The whole family is losing." Usually a complete overhaul of the entire family situation is in order, along with the use of some individualized nighttime discipline techniques which are beyond the scope of this book. If being the perfect nighttime parent wipes out your effectiveness during the day, you should recognize this as a red flag which indicates that you should seek help, the sooner the better.

Difficult decisions are often necessary in the growth of a new family. A realistic assessment and acceptance of your tolerance level is absolutely necessary for achieving the main benefit of the attachment style of parenting—enjoying your child. Sometimes you have to admit that the giver is worn out and has to rest a bit while dad or grandma or a loving friend meets the baby's needs.

Reference
Procaccini, J. and Kiefaber, M. W. 1983. *Parent Burnout.* Garden City, NY: Doubleday.

CHAPTER 11

The Shutdown Syndrome

I am becoming increasingly aware that there is a group of high need babies who show varying degrees of developmental delay as a reaction to receiving less attention than they need. The following are letters from two mothers whom I have recently counseled regarding developmental delay in their babies.

Letter One: The Effects of Crying It Out

"I am an experienced mother, but still was able to be swayed against my better judgment. Because Andy was so different from his two older siblings, I felt like all my experience almost didn't matter with him. I reread all of my baby and child care books, but found nothing telling me about the kind of baby Andy was.

"My first child was very ill as a baby. She didn't enjoy being held or rocked very much, as she was always in pain. She seemed to be able to stand only so much touching and stimulation before she would start crying uncontrollably. She weaned herself at nine months, much to my dismay. Our second child was normal in every respect. I carried her on my chest in a baby carrier. She fell asleep with me at night while nursing. Sometimes I'd lift her into her bassinet beside my bed, and sometimes I fell asleep and she never made it into the bassinet. She weaned herself at twelve months. Both of these babies were able to play well in the playpen if I had to do something for a short period and couldn't keep an eye on them.

"Then along came baby Andy. He was so cute and lovable. As a newborn he loved to fall asleep on my chest, listening to my breathing and heartbeat. I was very tired most of the time with a newborn and two other children under four years of age. Consequently Andy rarely made it into the bassinet beside my bed. He just slept with me. He was fun to hold, so I held him throughout the day. He never stiffened his body, leaned back, or wanted down. He just kind of molded his body to your lumps and bumps and held on.

"Andy grew very large quickly. He became too heavy to carry in the carrier, so I started pushing him in the stroller. He'd be happy in the stroller for five minutes, but then he'd start crying. He never stopped until I picked him up. He was getting too big for the bassinet. He was a restless sleeper, and this meant that if he was in bed with us the other two children couldn't have the cuddle time they needed as it would disturb him and make him cry. I was very tired, and in turn, found myself resenting the girls. So Andy went to his crib in the nursery at night where he had already been napping during the day. He wouldn't go to sleep in the nursery, not even with rocking. So I'd nurse him down to sleep in my bed first and then carry him in to the crib.

"When he started crawling I could no longer lay him beside me wherever I went—for example, just out of reach of the kitchen floor I was waxing. So I set up the playpen. Every time I put him in it, he got hysterical. I wasn't used to hearing him cry, so by the time I finished the floor or took a shower or whatever, I was a basket case.

"Andy was now old enough for solid food. He squirmed on my lap at the table, wanting to crawl up on the food and plates. So I put him in the high chair. He ate, played, and really enjoyed it, as long as I (not even Daddy) fed him and tended to his every need. If I left to fix dinner for us or even to get some more food for him, he would cry. If he cried, he would stop eating. People would say, 'He's really spoiled. He's got you wrapped around his little finger.' Or 'You've got real trouble on your hands. That's a temper tantrum he's throwing. You better spank him and get him into line before it's too late.'

"He now wanted to play and make noise during church, so it was time to take him to the nursery. It got to the point where they could hear me coming because Andy was already crying. I had to pry him off my body. Very gradually he became accustomed to one of the workers, but he had to be held the entire time, clinging to his little pillow from home. Since this was the pastor's son, I had plenty of well-meaning women of all ages offering advice: 'Give him more solid food' or 'Let him cry it out.' Most people seemed to think that unless I did something soon, Andy would grow up to be very clingy.

"The crowning blow came when I went to visit my dad and stepmother. I arrived there so proud of my baby and left feeling miserable and like a failure as a mother. My stepmom meant well and was trying to help, but ouch! She's a second grade teacher and has had lots of specialized training in dealing with young children. She witnessed some of Andy's crying episodes in the playpen. She told me that it was all my fault he was this way because I had catered to him too much as a newborn. She said it took me eight months to make him this way, so the problem wouldn't clear up overnight. She said he'd be fine and I should just leave him in the playpen where he was safe, as long as there were toys and he was dry. Who was I to argue with this expert? So I left the poor little thing there and went out front with Dad. I couldn't stand it for very long and came back in. Even though Andy was crying so pitifully and holding his arms up to me, she said, 'He's all right. There's no need for you to check on him.'

"Later, I called my pediatrician and told him about the crying episodes in the playpen and voiced the fears that my son would become a 'mama's boy.' The doctor advised me to leave Andy in the playpen and do my work around the house. He would eventually give up and quit crying. This was on a Monday. If Andy was still crying by Friday, I was to call back so we could figure out something else, since we couldn't leave him to cry for more than five or six days!

"The first day he never stopped crying. He'd be sopping wet with perspiration and would fall asleep exhausted. He would cry out in his sleep and wake himself up, and then he would start all over again. I couldn't stand it. It went against everything in me. I would cry. I would try to do housework, but I couldn't. I would go outside and cry out to God for direction or go in the bedroom, shut the door, and put a pillow over my head to muffle the sound. When I could no longer stand it, I would call a friend. She'd say, 'Now, Janet, you know what the doctor said. You didn't make him this way overnight, so it will take a while. Hang in there and stay tough.'

"On the second day, Andy actually made himself vomit. I couldn't eat that night I felt so awful. The next morning, as soon as I carried him into the front room and he saw the playpen, he started crying and vomited up all the breast milk from his last nursing. I decided, 'Forget this. I can't do this to him anymore.'

"From this point on, he seemed even more clingy. I'd put him in the high chair, and he would take only a few bites of food and then start crying. All he wanted to do was nurse, but he wouldn't even do that very often or for very long.

He had dropped from the seventieth percentile to the fortieth on the weight charts at his nine-month checkup. A month later he was down to the twentieth. The pediatrician sent us to the hospital for tests, all of which came out normal. A month later, Andy's weight had dropped off the charts. Four days before this last checkup, I had started sitting Andy on my lap during meals, letting him feed himself adult food off my plate instead of giving him one new bland baby food a week. He seemed more interested and ate more than usual. The pediatrician wanted to send us to an endocrinologist, but when I told him Andy had recently been eating better, he agreed to wait one more month. I had never told the pediatrician that I had given up on his advice to let Andy cry. I didn't want to look like a failure.

"I did not want to have to take Andy to a specialist. At this point, my husband and I asked the congregation to pray for Andy. A mother from church called me and suggested I listen to Dr. Sears's radio program. I tuned in to hear a mother asking a question about her high need baby, and he explained that 'Smart babies don't let their mothers put them down.' I had never known that there could be a baby like this, but as Dr. Sears explained more about high need babies, I knew I had one. I was so excited! Here was someone who knew about my baby. Maybe it wasn't my fault that he was like that!

"I thought back on how I had always had Andy with me. Then I realized that systematically, in the space of about one week, I had unknowingly pushed him away from me—from my arms into a stroller, from my bed into a crib in another room, from my lap to a high chair, from keeping him moving with me into a playpen by himself. The crowning blow was letting him cry it out, all by himself. I was saddened that I had not heard the radio program earlier. It could have saved me worry and grief, not to mention money and trauma at the hospital. I realized that it was after I had let Andy cry for so long that he had stopped eating and started losing weight.

"I started thinking of him as a high need baby. I bought a back-pack baby carrier. We became inseparable. I carried him everywhere. Whether I was doing dishes or talking on the phone, Andy was on my back. I never put him in the high chair. He ate on my lap. I nursed him to sleep in my bed. (He had always enjoyed kneading my stomach with his toes.) At night I got him out of his crib and into our bed for his 11:00 p.m. feeding. This was followed by a long cuddle time with us, with lots of touching and little sounds which he would make back to us. He loved it. Then I would put him back in his crib so the other two children wouldn't wake him when they came bumbling into our bed between 3:00 and 6:00 a.m.

"I sold our stroller and purchased one of the new types that allowed Andy to face me while I pushed him. I could talk to him to reassure him and reach out and touch him when he needed it.

"The more little intimacies I initiated with him, the more he began to eat. The happier he was, the less clingy he became. At his next weight check, he had gained four pounds and was now back on the chart. He's definitely on the upswing now.

"After another month, Andy had really changed. He gained another two-and-a-half pounds. His face is wide and masculine again, and he has cute little creases in his thighs. His appetite for food and breastfeeding is excellent. He even takes his feedings in a high chair. He is good-natured again, laughs a lot, and enjoys life. Around new people or with babysitters he still becomes very listless or cries continually until I show up on the scene. I don't have to back-pack him around the house anymore. But if I go more than ten or fifteen feet away, he dissolves into a little heap on the floor, gives up, and cries pitifully. So I do still have to carry him from room to room. He is happy playing with his big sisters, as long as the play centers on him. I can even put him in the dreaded playpen now while I shower—that is, if I make it a quick shower and have given him his allotted amount of attention for the day.

"We will have to keep up the extra attention, touching, cuddling, and nursing. Andy needs to be included in every part of our family life. He can't be left out just because he's a baby. We have even been able to let our three- and five-year-old get in on this. They enjoy massaging him, stroking his hair, and singing to him. He gets very excited and loves them very much."

Letter Two: Babies Need Attention

"The doctor advised me to stop giving Jennifer so much attention. He said to let her be by herself. He said that she should be in bed by 7:00 p.m. and we should let her cry herself to sleep. We were not to rock her to sleep anymore. If she awoke during the night, we were to let her cry herself back to sleep and not go to her or let her sleep with us.

"Jennifer became very withdrawn and insecure. She would panic every time I left the room and continue crying even when I came back. She would sit on the floor and stare into space and seem disinterested in everything. She was regressing and wasn't making any efforts to learn anything. We followed the doctor's advice and let her scream herself to sleep. When she would wake up we didn't make any attempts to comfort her.

"At this point, we didn't know what to do. We were very upset because Jennifer was withdrawn and unsettled. I should have listened to my instinct; I didn't feel right about following the doctor's advice. Finally my grandmother found you, Dr. Sears, and that was an answer to my prayers. Your advice was just what we needed.

"My husband and I followed your instructions to the letter. We did everything you advised. We didn't let Jennifer cry herself to sleep anymore. We rocked her and let her sleep with us. I carried her around most of the day, played with her, and gave her a lot of my time and attention.

"I saw results within two days. Jennifer perked up and was much happier, more alert, and seemed to want to learn. She learned how to clap, and she slept all night for the first time in months. I rocked her to sleep and allowed her to stay in bed all night with us. She stirred a couple of times, but when she realized we were there, she would grab for my hand and hold it and go back to sleep. We gave her home-cooked meals and ground them fresh for her and discontinued buying her jarred foods. She responded very well and became secure and trusting again. My husband was very attentive to her and started to rock her to sleep as he had done before. After a month of this, she was a very happy and secure baby again. She was her old self, laughing and playful."

What Happened?

These are two examples of what happens when nature's design for mother-infant attachment is not followed. I believe that every baby comes wired with a critical level of need for touching and holding. If the need is met, the baby has a greater chance of reaching his developmental potential. If it is not met, he runs the risk of varying degrees of developmental delay or shutdown. The babies in these two cases showed obvious and measurable effects of shutdown. I wonder how many high need babies receiving a level of care that is not adequate for them show subtle effects of shutdown which go undetected.

Part of the shutdown syndrome may be the result of reactive depression. The baby is grieving over the loss of an important relationship, just as adults show physical and emotional changes in reaction to a loss. This reactive depression is carried one step farther when the baby's signals are not listened to. Crying is the strongest attachment-promoting behavior a baby has. Can you imagine the depth of grief which overtakes a little person whose cries are not listened to and who possesses limited abilities to compensate for this loss?

Many medical studies demonstrate the beneficial effects of parent-infant attachment on infant development. A complete review is beyond the scope of this book, but it appears that every organ system is affected, for better or worse, by the degree of touching and holding the infant receives. Some babies with very high needs (such as those described in the previous letters) may shut down their total system in reaction to a restrained response to their needs. A baby who has been let down may shut down.

References

Geber, M. 1958. The psycho-motor development of African children in the first year and influences of maternal behavior. *J Soc Psychol* 47:185.

Klaus, M. and Kennell, J. 1976. *Maternal-Infant Bonding*. St. Louis: C. V. Mosby.

Montagu, A. 1971. *Touching: The Human Significance of the Skin*. New York: Harper and Row.

CHAPTER 12

Disciplining the High Need Child

"He's so stubborn, he just won't mind," complained the mother of a high need two-year-old. Because every child is unique and because every parent has his or her own style, there are as many methods of discipline as there are high need children. In this chapter I will present a style of discipline that has worked well in our family and in other families in my practice. Because high need children are notoriously resistant to punishment as a discipline technique, the goal of this chapter is to help parents create the atmosphere and attitudes that make punishment less necessary. When punishment is necessary, this chapter will help you make sure it is appropriately administered.

Why High Need Children Are More Difficult to Discipline

The temperament traits that may be an asset to the older high need child are the same ones that get the young child into trouble. Because these children are so intense, they go at things in a big way and tackle tasks that are beyond their developmental capabilities. Many a worn-out mother has spent the day chasing behind her high need child who is trying to rearrange the entire house. These children tend to be impulsive; they rush headlong into a curious situation or after a desired object without stopping first to form a game plan. This impulsiveness leads them into trouble. These children, because they are so acutely aware of their environment, are intensely curious. They want to catch anything that moves, turn anything that turns, and push anything that will go. They are quick to protest when their exploring is restricted. High need children are not known for their caution. They tend to be climbers and hangers and are the children most likely to dart out into the street because something interesting is on the other side.

"He's so defiant," complained a worn-out mother who has shouted "no" a thousand times and is becoming frustrated with her child's refusal to get the point. Many high need children have a strong ego which clashes with their caregivers. "I do it myself" is their battle cry. Inner pride, confidence, and assertiveness are characteristic especially of high need children who are products of the attachment style of parenting which builds up a child's self-esteem. Other methods of child rearing that encourage parents not to give in to their child's needs and demands squelch the high need child's personality development and cause him not to trust his environment. This can lead to fragile self-esteem.

Here's how the impulsive mind of the high need toddler processes your "no." A curious and impulsive toddler does not yet have the wisdom to discern which knobs are harmful and which are not. He wants to touch the dangerous knob. When "no" follows the first reach toward the knob by approximately one millisecond, he soon learns that "no" means he should stop his actions, especially if the "no" is accompanied by picking the child up, removing him from the knob, and admonishing him with "Don't touch. That will hurt Johnny!" Children with easier temperaments get the point rather quickly; all the parent has to do is look at the child sternly, and this docile toddler melts into swift compliance. High need children, on the other hand, need stronger "law enforcement" accompanying the no. This child needs to be picked up immediately, looked squarely in the eye, and authoritatively removed from the dangerous situation. The parent may have to repeat this admonition many times before the child gets the point. Each time the "no" may need to be accompanied by stronger admonishments, but the child will eventually get the point.

Patience.   It is easy to become frustrated when you feel that you're just not getting through to your child. But don't give up. You *are* getting through to your child, but it takes longer to shape the will of high need children. This is why the early months of taking charge of the fussy baby are so important. The trusting relationship established then lays the foundation for the effectiveness of discipline when the confrontation of wills begins. The attachment style of parenting allows you to be more firm with your child because you and your child are operating from a basis of trust.

Parents who have developed a strong sensitivity toward their child will discover that the child also develops a sensitivity to parents' moods. Discipline problems are most likely to occur during times of parental stress, when parent and child are not in harmony with each other. Parents have often told me, "When I'm feeling good, my child is good."

Tantrums.   Most high need children are prone to temper tantrums between one and two years of age. They protest violently at any infringement upon their impulsive behavior. The temper tantrums in most seemingly unruly children are the result of two feelings: the child's own inability to conform to the will of another and his anger at being out of control.

These children are ambivalent. They have strong impulses but lack the inner controls to handle them. The high need toddler wants to do more than he is able to do. Tantrums are often a manifestation of a child's anger with himself and with the world around him. The toddler does not have the verbal skills to express and communicate his anger so he does so in actions. The most terrifying of all tantrums, both to parent and to child, are breath-holding spells in which the child cries so hard and becomes so angry that toward the end of the cry he appears to hold his breath, turns blue, becomes limp, and seems to be on the verge of fainting. Fortunately, just when parents are on the verge of frantic helplessness, the child resumes breathing. He does no harm to himself but leaves his parents a wreck. Mothers of high need children will often describe the tantrum behavior as "becoming unglued." Keeping your child from falling apart and gluing him back together again is one of the most frustrating tasks for parents of high need children.

"She Turned on Me"

"My one-and-a-half-year-old and I were very close. We were together from birth. She nursed on demand and slept with me. We've had a wonderful relationship. But now she's started hitting, kicking, and biting me."

This mother had recently returned to work part-time, largely because of peer pressure rather than her own desire or necessity. The baby was reacting to the loss of the strong attachment to her mother; she was angry because the bond was being loosened before she was ready. The greater the attachment, the stronger the grief reaction. Once mother returned to full-time mothering, the child's aggressive behavior stopped. High need babies are capable of strong attachments, but they are also more sensitive when those attachments are threatened.

If brought up in an environment that complements their temperamental traits, high need children become strong personalities. Though this is ultimately a positive trait, inner strength of personality makes a child prone to defiance and merits him the label of "a strong-willed child." The "I want" in his personality is often perceived by parents as "I won't." For example, a two-year-old happily playing at his friend's house feels so right and fits so well within the current situation that he protests loudly when mother comes in and announces that it is time to go. This child deeply wants to continue doing what he's doing and does not easily yield his will to that of another. His protests comes across as "I won't." The mother perceives this as defiance and tries to assert her rightful role as authority figure. A clash of wills ensues, and a no-win situation develops. There is a fine line between the "I don't *want* to" of a normal strong-willed personality and the "I *won't* do it" of a defiant child. The hardest thing about disciplining a high need child is instilling a healthy respect for authority in the child without squelching the strength of his will. Dr. James Dobson calls this dilemma, "Shaping the will without breaking the spirit."

An Approach to Disciplining the High Need Child

Parents often confuse discipline with punishment. Punishment is an external force, applied because the child has strayed from the straight and narrow path. Punishment is really only one form of discipline. I wish parents to think of discipline primarily as direction from within the child that motivates him to stay on the path because he feels right when he acts right and does not feel right when he acts wrongly.

High need children are notoriously resistant to external punishment, especially corporal punishment or spanking. Thus the most important disciplinary goal for the parents of a high need child is the creation of an attitude *within* the child that will motivate him in the right direction. Along with this, parents need to create an atmosphere in the home that makes punishment less necessary. Children don't always know what's best for them, especially high need children, and there will be times when punishment is necessary. It is vital that punishment is appropriately administered.

Creating the Attitude and the Atmosphere

Toward the end of a child's first year, the parents' role as nurturer expands into that of an authority figure and designer of a safe environment. A strong authority figure is absolutely necessary in disciplining all children, especially high need children. A child must know for certain who's in charge.

Authority figures.   How do you become a strong authority figure? The early chapters of this book have stressed the importance of the attachment style of parenting and being open and responsive to your child's cues. This builds up a trusting relationship between parent and child. Trust is the basis of authority. When the impulsive toddler goes after the knob on the gas stove and you descend upon him with an authoritarian ''no,'' you are demanding that your child yield his will to yours. He must trust you unconditionally in order to do this. The stronger the child's will, the greater the amount of trust required.

''But how do I handle these tantrums?'' is the plea of the helpless parent. I don't believe in ignoring tantrums because these children are out of control and expect someone in authority to help them regain control. You cannot handle these temper tantrums for the child, but you certainly can help. I have found it most helpful to hold the struggling child firmly and lovingly with your arms around him, restraining his flailing arms. Accompany this with a reassuring voice saying, ''You are out of control, and Daddy is just going to hold you tight until you feel better.'' Even the most defiant child will usually turn down his runaway engine and submit to someone more in control. He will melt into your arms as if thanking you for rescuing him from himself.

When disciplining the high need child, use lots of eye contact. This body language tells the child that you are truly talking from your heart and that you are disciplining him because you love him. When you finally get through to high need children, they develop respect for your fairness about their discipline. This approach to discipline is not lenient or permissive. It requires wisdom and the investment of time.

Realistic Expectations

Disciplining the high need child requires that you have realistic expectations of what your child can cope with. You should not impose demands on a child that are beyond his temperament's ability to handle. Expecting an impulsive toddler to walk down the aisle of a supermarket without grabbing all those tempting delights is totally unrealistic. Parents of high need children usually are more accepting of a wider spectrum of their child's behavior. They chalk up the small problems to their child's personality and avoid high risk situations such as supermarkets which usually bring out the worst in parent and child.

If taking your child to the supermarket is unavoidable, be prepared to be creative in your discipline by playing games such as "Mommy's Helper." Show your child what you want to get off the shelf, and let him grab it and put it into the basket for you. Give him lots of recognition for his help. This does take more time, but one of the biggest obstacles to establishing harmony with a high need child is the pressure of time and deadlines.

Spanking

"I can't get him to mind. The harder I spank, the worse he gets," complained a frustrated mother. In my experience, high need children resist the effects of corporal punishment. Spanking is supposed to operate on the behavior modification principle of reinforcement: An undesirable action receives an undesirable reaction—a spanking. High need children often do not make the connection between the action

and the response and as a result regard spanking as confusing and unfair. For many children, discovering that turning on the stove will be followed by punishment convinces
them to leave the stove alone. However, the consequences
of wrong actions don't sink in with other children. They are
not being willfully stubborn; they just don't get the message.
Some ultrasensitive children may not only fail to connect a
spanking with the behavior, they may even connect its negative effect with the person giving it. Spanking may be justified as an emotional reaction in life-threatening situations
(such as riding a tricycle into a busy street) and will be effective because the child will get the message that you have
his safety in mind, but other methods of discipline are usually
much more effective for the high need child.

CHAPTER 13

The Pay-Off

"It's been a long, tough struggle, but we're finally beginning to cash in on our investment," explained the parents of a high need two-year-old. In no other aspect of child care is the investment/return ratio as high as in parenting the high need child. One hot day as I was writing this book I looked at the bottle of the beverage I was drinking. It read, "No deposit, no return." This message is also true of parenting the high need child.

The child helps to develop the parent. When parents are open to their baby's temperament, accept his needs, and develop a parenting style which works for the whole family, they bring out the best in the child. The response from the child in turn brings out the best in the parents. This mutual giving causes the entire parent-child relationship to operate at a higher level. Good things happen to parents and children when they grow up in harmony with each other.

The Outcome

Parents will often ask, "How will my child turn out? Is he going to be a hyperactive child? Will he ever leave our bed? Will he ever wean?" High need children vary greatly, but an analysis of the cases of high need babies that I have run into shows some general trends.

High need babies can indeed become a joy to their parents. Their behavior is channeled into positive personality traits. The parenting styles used in the group of high need infants with good outcomes have several features in common:

Unrestricted breastfeeding for a minimum of two years.

Openness and responsiveness to baby's cries, cues, and temperament.

Sharing sleep with parents for at least two years.

An involved and supportive father.

Parents who are involved in support systems which affirm their parenting choices.

The high need children whose parents followed these guidelines became sensitive, caring, trusting, fearless individuals.

Problem Baby, Problem Child?

To help answer the question of whether difficult babies turn out to be problem children, two researchers began the New York Longitudinal Study in 1956 (Thomas et al 1968). They followed 136 children from early infancy into later childhood. They attempted to categorize the infants as either easy or difficult based upon nine categories of temperament: activity level, rhythmicity of biologic functions, ease of adaptability, approach-withdrawal reactions to new situations, sensory threshold, mood (primarily positive or negative mood), intensity of mood, distractibility, and persistence or attention span. The easy child in their study was characterized by biologic regularity, an easy approach to new situations, a generally positive mood, and adaptability. The difficult children in the study showed biologic irregularity, usually withdrew from new situations, had many negative moods and expressed them with marked intensity, and were slow to adapt to change.

The results of this study showed that infants labeled as difficult babies exhibited a higher incidence of behavior disorders as older children, mainly in the areas of sleep, mood, discipline, and peer relationships. While the study did show a correlation between infant behavior and later difficulties, it was not a perfect correlation. Easy babies did sometimes turn out to be difficult children and vice versa. The authors concluded only that difficult babies are at higher risk of becoming more difficult children.

While the researchers did not intend to judge the effects of different parenting styles, the study did show that no one parenting style worked with every child all the time. The most successful parent-child relationship was one in which the mother showed both consistency and flexibility and used a combination of attitudes and practices in her parenting. This ties in with the style of attachment parenting which is advocated throughout this book. The babies with the best outcome were the ones whose mothers were flexible in responding to their needs. The study showed that the child with the good outcome was often the product of parents who never considered him to have a behavioral disturbance; they felt instead that the child's troublesome behavior was the expression of his own personality, which needed modifying. The child who had a poor outcome was the product of parenting styles which were excessively stressful, inconsistent, and confusing to the child.

Benefits of Attachment Parenting for High Need Children

Enhanced Development

High need babies who are in harmony with their environment often reach developmental milestones sooner. There
is an energy-sparing effect on the baby because the parents
provide harmony in the baby's environment. This prevents
the baby from wasting energy overcoming his own internal
stress and allows him to use that energy to develop his skills.
Researchers who have studied infant care patterns in other
cultures have made some interesting observations about infants reared in almost continuous contact with their mothers
(Geber 1958). These mothers carry their babies with them
in slings. The babies are given free access to the breast and
seem to nurse continuously. These babies are constantly in
somebody's arms because when mother's arms wear out the
extended family is around to play "pass the baby." The babies seldom cry because their needs are anticipated and
promptly responded to. Babies and mothers sleep together
and nurse through the night. The researchers noticed that
infants who received this attachment style of parenting were
clearly precocious in both neuromuscular and cognitive development when compared with infants of more "advanced"
cultures.

On the other hand, babies who grow up in a less satisfying environment are often slower in their emotional and motor development. This phenomenon is known in pediatric
circles as the "deprivation syndrome."

I can tell a lot about the strength of the parent-child attachment by observing the toddler at play. Picture two toddlers in a playroom with their mothers. The high need toddler
who is not strongly attached to his parents will often flit from
toy to toy, spending very little time with any one toy. He has
a poor attention span and seldom acknowledges his mother.
The high need child of attachment parents also flits from toy
to toy, but he studies them more attentively and periodically

checks into home base (mother or father) for reassurance that all is well. Both toddlers are showing independence, but the detached toddler's independence lacks direction. The attached toddler learns more from his explorations. He is more secure and free to explore the unknown because of his attachment to his parents.

Giving Children

High need babies who are matched with giving parents become giving children. Good takers later become good givers because giving is the style they are accustomed to. These children share more easily—something which comes hard to many children. They also seem more concerned about the needs and rights of the other children around them. Their parents have achieved a healthy balance in their giving, neither overindulging nor restraining. This is in contrast to so-called "spoiled" children who are often the products of inappropriate giving, either too much or too little.

Sensitivity

Because high need babies have grown up in an environment where their caregivers were sensitive to their needs, they become children who are more sensitive to the needs of other children. A crying baby or another child getting hurt bothers these children. Why? Because that is the response they learned when they were crying and hurting. Parents are the prime recipients of this sensitivity. One mother shared with me the story of how on a particularly down day she was crying. Her three-year-old daughter (a former high need baby) hurried over, put her arms around her mother, and said from her heart, "Don't cry, Mommy. I'll help you."

Feeling Right

When harmony is achieved between a high need baby and giving parents, a feeling of inner rightness overtakes the child and becomes part of his nature. These children exude a feel-

"What About the Other Kids?"

"Katie, who is four years old, has weathered the storm with some interesting effects. She did not know any other baby before Megan, our high need baby, so she came to assume that every baby was like Megan. This became evident when she played with her dolls. The dolls always cried a lot, and she always comforted them as I did Megan. She would hold them and rock or nurse them and repeat my exact words, 'Come on, honey. Don't cry, Mommy's here.' Katie was often involved in soothing and quieting her dolls. This was a wonderful sight for me to witness.

"Then a close friend had a baby who was the epitome of perfect. He hardly ever cries, never gets upset, and never screams. Katie asked why our baby couldn't be more like the other baby. I felt bad, but I could certainly understand her question.

"At least this experience has given her a realistic expectation of what babies can be like some of the time. It has also shown her that we don't abandon each other in times of need, no matter how frustrated we are. In her play I see that she has mastered some mothering techniques that I had to learn by trial and error. I hope that mothering will be easier for her because of this, especially if she has a high need infant."

Parents may wonder how a fussy baby affects the older children in the family. Do they grow up thinking that all babies are fussy? This story is a good example of how an older child picks up on mother's modeling. It was important that Katie learn that not all babies are fussy like her little sister; otherwise there could be a damaging effect on her attitude towards motherhood. From watching her own mother, Katie has learned to be a giving person.

ing of peace, as if they are right for their world and the world is right for them. A peaceful child is better able to handle the many stresses that will come his way during his normal growth and development. He will continually strive to regain this feeling of rightness by modifying his temperament and his environment accordingly. The child who has grown up from infancy continually not feeling right is at a higher risk for becoming a generally angry child, the type who seems always to have a chip on his shoulder.

Direction

Demanding babies often become impulsive children, and it is this unbridled impulsiveness that gets them in trouble. Parents will often ask if their fussy baby is likely to become a hyperactive child. Most parents of hyperactive children do report that they "came wired this way." Yes, fussy babies do have a higher chance of becoming hyperactive children. This is where the parents' perseverance in gentling their high need baby really pays off. Children whose parents helped them learn control in early infancy seem to have more control of themselves later on.

Parents who have practiced the attachment style of parenting know their hyperactive child so well that they are better able to channel the child's impulsive and destructive behavior. Without this foundation, parents flounder in a sea of uncertainty, and their child is turned over to the advice of specialists and experts rather than being guided by intuitive parents. Hyperactive children who do not have the foundation of attachment parenting are often very angry, though this may not be evident on the surface. I feel that anger is one of the most overlooked feelings behind most behavior problems. In my experience the most difficult hyperactive child to deal with is one who operates from a basis of anger. One of my goals in writing this book is to help children avoid feeling angry. Fussy babies who are destined to be hyperactive children, but who have received attachment parenting, operate from a basis of trust rather than anger.

Fearlessness

Parents often describe high need children as fearless because they have grown up in an environment where fear was avoided at all costs. "She has no need to fear," said one mother who devoted a great deal of energy to creating a peaceful environment around her high need baby. When the fears inevitable in later childhood arrive, her child will have the resources to handle these fears.

Trust

If you were to ask me to use one word to describe the high need baby who has grown up in a harmonious environment, I would choose the word "trusting." When an infant is trusted, he learns to trust. When a high need baby grows up in a responsive environment he learns to believe that his needs should and will be properly identified and consistently met. This represents two kinds of trust: The infant trusts that his cues are worthy of being listened to, and he trusts that his caregivers will respond to these cues. As a result the infant feels that because his cues are noticed, he is a special person, and the caregivers who respond are special also. Both parents and child profit by simply listening to each other.

Self-Esteem

All of the above traits of high need children can be summed up by the term self-esteem. These harmoniously parented babies feel right about themselves and feel like they fit into their environment. They eventually turn out to be creative children who give back to their environment more of what their environment gave to them. They make our world a more interesting and peaceful place to live.

Benefits for Parents

There are times, I'm sure, when parents feel that there is absolutely no advantage in having a high need baby. They seem somewhat surprised when I use positive terms such as "blessed with" and "fortunate," but I mean them sincerely. High need babies, properly parented, can bring out the best in their parents. Parents of high need babies receive a good return on their investment of time and energy.

Knowing the Child Better

By being tuned into their infant's cues, showing unrestrained responses, and evaluating the feedback the infant gives them, parents come to know their child better. They learn what works and what doesn't work. Even mothers who begin their parenting career with shaky intuition gradually become more confident when they go along with the conditions (the attachment style of parenting) that allow their intuition to mature. This confidence is boosted regularly by responses from the infant, and the whole system of parent-child supply and demand operates at a higher, more harmonious level. In

---

"Other Mothers Seem to Have More Control"

"Why can't I handle my baby? I can't get him to stop crying or go to sleep or get on a schedule. I can't put him down and leave him like other mothers can. Other mothers seem more in control of their babies than I am. Why are other mothers better at this?"

Don't compare your baby with other babies. How easy the baby is to handle does not reflect your effectiveness as a mother. Your baby fusses as much as he does primarily because of his own temperament, not because of your mothering abilities. Mothers tend to exaggerate the "goodness" of their babies, and you may be seeing these other mothers' babies only at their good times. Remember the parent-child law of supply and demand: your baby demands so much because he needs so much. His demands are geared to bring out the best in his caregivers so that his temperament can develop in the right direction.

---

short, parents become more sensitive. Mother and father often become more sensitive to each other as well, and their marriage prospers. A stable and fulfilled marriage gives parenting the high need baby a real head start.

Greater Acceptance

Attachment parents develop more acceptance of their child's behavior. In addition to building up your sensitivity, you build up your tolerance for this demanding, draining child. This starts with developing realistic expectations of your child's behavior instead of comparing him with other babies. Your child does not behave like the child next door because he is *not* the child next door. This acceptance of your child's behavior gradually matures into being able to focus more on the positive aspects of his temperament. This comes from having worked so hard to modify the negatives and accentuate the positives. I find that parents of high need children gradually come to use fewer negative terms in describing their child. The baby graduates from being unpredictable, uncontentable, and unsatisfied and becomes challenging, interesting, curious, aware, confident, and bright. Some labels such as exhausting and draining seem to stick with high need children, because they are above-average children and require more than the average amount of energy to keep them going. I have noticed that mothers who have both survived and thrived with their high need babies seem to get a "second wind" every six months or so. This extra boost of energy sees them through those especially trying times when a child is in transition from one developmental stage to the next.

Easier Discipline

Because parents know their child, they tend to provide discipline by following the intuitive leadings of their hearts rather than choosing a general disciplinary method out of a book and trying their hardest to make the child conform. Parents of high need children seem to read their children better. They anticipate those situations which get the child in trouble and intuitively and creatively channel the child's impulses into alternative behavior. Because the child feels right, he is more likely to act right. Discipline is easier for parents who have been in harmony with their child because they have worked hard to create an attitude within their child and an atmosphere within their home that make punishment less necessary.

Enjoying the Child

All these benefits help you enjoy your child more. Helping you enjoy your child is one of the main goals of attachment parenting and of THE GROWING FAMILY SERIES. When parents and child are in harmony with each other, they do seem to bring out the best in one other. As a father of a high need child once said to me, "Nothing matures a parent more than getting in harmony with a high need child." I think the term maturity meant more to this father than extra grey hairs.

Modeling

The real pay-off in the parenting of a high need child comes because you are modeling a style of parenting and behavior for your child. Parents, keep in mind that you are bringing up someone else's future husband or wife, father or mother. The parenting styles which your child learns from you are the ones he is most likely to follow when he becomes a parent.

Modeling of parenting styles can even get through to teenagers. One day my wife and I were sitting in our family room when we heard our nine-month-old daughter, Erin, crying in our bedroom. Since we believe in responding to our baby's cries, we got up and walked toward the bedroom door. As we got near the door, we heard the cries stop. Curious, we looked in to see why Erin had stopped crying, and what we saw left a warm feeling in our hearts: Jim, our sixteen-year-old athlete, was lying next to Erin, stroking her and gentling her. Why did Jim do this? Because he was following our modeling that when babies cry, someone should listen and respond.

References

Geber, M. 1958. The psycho-motor development of African children in the first year and influences of maternal behavior. *J Soc Psychol* 47:185.

Thomas, A. et al. 1968. *Temperament and Behavior Disorders in Children*. New York: New York University Press.

CHAPTER 14

Jonathan: A Case History

This is the story of Jonathan, a thriving high need child, and his parents Bob and Nancy, who have managed to survive those first difficult years. Nancy tells the story.

"I was so excited to find out I was pregnant. I had 'done my thing' as far as study and travel and now was ready to settle down to raise a family. Generally, my pregnancy was a real joy, but there were periods when I felt ambivalent about having a baby. I had always wanted to have a baby and part of me was excited, but that part was sometimes buried under confusion, anxiety, and an occasional feeling of being trapped. Two years earlier I had suffered a miscarriage, and I was worried it might happen again. It was hard to believe a real baby would result from all this. I think this all contributed to my feeling inadequate about handling the pregnancy and birth. I felt afraid and powerless.

"Bob and I decided that we needed to be committed to the concept of a family and to each other. We had to dive, as it were, into the whole idea of parenthood, taking it as it came and being willing to sacrifice as necessary. We both made that commitment and to this day we are still involved with it.

"Around the fourth month of my pregnancy, Jonathan started his rumble-tumble act. I knew I had a live wire on my hands, but I didn't realize that all this activity would be so prophetic. I noticed that the baby would respond to sound, physical activity, and my stressful emotions with strong kicking. In fact, if I used the adding machine in the office where I was working, he would kick so hard I had to stop.

"Like many pregnant women, I filled my life with all the baby books I could get my hands on. Bob and I dutifully enrolled in a husband-coached childbirth class and practiced our daily exercises faithfully. As the due date got closer, I became increasingly anxious about the birth. I had read books and seen TV shows where women died in childbirth or sounded as if they were dying. My mother had told me that labor was the most painful, unnatural thing she had ever gone through. I was tired of hearing all those horror stories.

"My labor was traumatic, complicated, and resulted in a cesarean. Bob later confided that because of this medical complication he was initially quite resentful of this little being who had brought his wife so close to disaster. He had to make a conscious effort during the bonding time we had studied and planned for. He knew we would never get those moments back. Even though my delivery did not go as hoped for, I was able to hold Jonathan in the recovery room within a half hour after birth. I began breastfeeding right away and, with Bob's help, Jonathan was with me a lot in the hospital as I recovered from the cesarean. Bob and I have since reflected on those first few days of spending time together as a family, and we feel they were vital for our becoming attached to Jonathan and overcoming our disappointment with the traumatic birth.

"Our first night at home was not at all as I had expected. I guess Jonathan decided it was time to begin my training program. I had naively expected to have a feeding schedule as in the hospital, but Jonathan, of course, had other ideas. I couldn't understand why he would not stay asleep when I put him in the crib. Despite my confusion, I was committed to not letting my baby cry, so we spent the night together on the living room couch where I fell asleep sitting up with Jonathan at my breast. When I woke four hours later, still sitting in the same position with my baby safe in my arms, I was horrified that I had fallen asleep holding him, but I also worried that he might begin to prefer sleeping with me rather than learning to sleep in his crib. I did not notice the fact that after spending those peaceful hours in my arms, he was calm enough that I could put him in his crib.

"This pattern continued through our first weeks, and I began to realize that Jonathan exhibited more than the normal demands of a newborn. I was baffled at my baby's reluctance to remain alone in his crib and his constant need to nurse. Intellectually I was prepared to breastfeed, but emotionally I was uncertain whether I was willing to sit and nurse all day—and night. Someone told me that tiny babies just ate and slept. My baby just ate. I dreamed of bottles, particularly at night. Jonathan was thriving, but I was languishing. Bob said I was surviving on hormones alone. Breastfeeding honestly did help. It forced me, the compulsive cleaner, to sit down with Jonathan whenever he needed to nurse.

"Besides his non-stop nursing, Jonathan needed non-stop motion. When he was six weeks old, he was no longer content just to lie in my arms. He would not be comforted unless he was being held, carried, rocked, or driven. After Bob came home from work, we took turns walking our son. Bob rocked while I slept. I could not have survived without him.

"My friends kept saying that Jonathan would grow out of it. He didn't. His cries became more intense. I was particularly frustrated by Jonathan's inconsistency in being comforted. What worked one day did not work the next. Some days nothing would satisfy his needs. He did not always find us comforting, but we were better than nothing. I would wonder whether I should give in and pick him up. But while I was thinking, 'Stop screaming and I'll hold you,' Jonathan seemed to be feeling, 'Hold me and I'll stop screaming.' During his clingy times he would look at me as if thinking, 'Do something!' It was a very frustrating situation for me as a parent to be in.

"My training as a teacher in child development kept haunting me. Erik Erikson's stages of social-emotional growth of the child begin with the stage of trust versus mistrust. Jonathan would either learn to trust his environment or learn varying degrees of mistrust. Even if we could not always alleviate Jonathan's discomfort, we could at least hold him and rock him and let him know that we cared. Even if he didn't always settle, he would still be learning trust.

"I felt so tied down. I could do nothing without Jonathan, and no one but me (and Bob when he was home) could care for him. I would get angry at him for being so difficult and then get angry and confused at myself, wondering if I had done something that made him this way. I would oscillate between feeling that I was doing something wrong and knowing that what I was doing was right. For the first time in my life I could understand how someone might abuse a child, and that scared me. My fatigue gave me a short fuse. When Bob got home, boy, did he get it if he stepped out of line. Bob would help calm Jonathan as best he could. I am so grateful that my husband believes in sharing the practical aspects of parenting our children, not just their conception.

"During the first few months I read every book I could find on babies and talked to other mothers and to our pediatrician. I found little information on fussy babies, and much of the advice I found was not right for my baby. By the time Jonathan was four months old, I felt as if I was at the end of my rope. I was angry and tired of reading and hearing that by some magical date he would get over it, sleep through the night, and calm down.

"My friends and relatives seemed equally baffled by Jonathan's behavior. My friends told me to get away from my baby. La Leche League suggested I take him with me. He was too fussy to leave and too fussy to take. Older women, including my mother, innocently suggested that I just put him in his playpen and let him learn to play independently. My milk was often thought to be the culprit. I got so tired of hearing, 'Give him a bottle' and 'Maybe you don't have enough milk.' Some suggested that he had colic, and it would be over by three months. People of the 'cry it out' persuasion and the babysitter-a-week philosophy descended upon us, warning that we were raising a child with terminal dependence who would be unable to grow and make decisions. Worst of all, they told us that Jonathan would be just plain spoiled.

"By now I had become very defensive about my mothering abilities. I was tired of the subtle suggestions that I was causing my baby's fussiness. I knew in my heart that I was a good mother, yet this advice did bother me.

Responding to a baby's needs builds an unbreakable bond of love and understanding.

"The biggest lessons Bob and I had to learn were to ignore standard baby care advice and to do whatever worked the best at the time, even if it seemed unorthodox. Early on we discarded concepts such as babysitters, weaning at six months, and easily enforced bedtime rituals.

"Once we determined that our rather unorthodox method of raising Jonathan was indeed the course set before us, we wanted others to understand the reasons for our decisions. We learned firsthand, however, that no issue divides adults as quickly as variations in child-raising techniques and philosophies. We learned to pick our friends and supporters carefully. It would have been easier to give in and go along with the standard advice, but our advisors did not know Jonathan. We found the most helpful and affirming advice in the book *Creative Parenting* and the most valuable support in our La Leche League group. It was such a relief to have someone affirm my mothering efforts.

"My greatest enemy in caring for Jonathan during the first year was lack of sleep. Once I discarded the fantasy that he would sleep in his crib and brought him into bed with us, we both slept better. Jonathan and I have fallen into the same sleep pattern. He usually awakens two or three times a night, but now I almost always find myself waking up about thirty seconds before he does. I will then nurse him as soon as he begins to stir, and in a few minutes we both are back to sleep. He is two years old, and this is our usual nighttime pattern.

"Usually I feel rested in the morning and not overly tired during the day. Not all nights are like this, however. Teething pain, separation anxiety, and minor illnesses sometimes throw a wrench into Jonathan's sleep patterns. I've learned that when Jonathan wakes me out of a sound sleep or is awakening four or more times during the night, something is bothering him. Unfortunately, I am not at my most sympathetic at four o'clock in the morning. When I have been up half the night, I have a hard time looking at his feelings instead of my own tired ones. But then, I guess this is a problem that all parents face at times, regardless of where their baby sleeps. Of all the ways to comfort an unhappy baby, I think that lying down and nursing is certainly the easiest. The biggest plus of all is that I really enjoy having Jonathan cuddled up next to me at night. I am so glad that I didn't miss out on this special closeness with him.

"After several good nights in a row, I feel energetic and loving and don't mind devoting most of my time to him. After a few wakeful nights, however, I become resentful, short-tempered, and self-pitying. Panicky thoughts invade my mind: 'He's never going to let me have a second baby' or 'This lack of sleep is going to kill me!' Sometimes I just lie there and cry.

"By morning things don't seem quite as bad. When I'm exhausted the best thing to do is simplify my day and concentrate on Jonathan's and my immediate needs. I have learned to ask Bob for help when I am tired—with cooking dinner, for example. It has been a big help when he has offered to take us out for a while, even if it is just for a short walk. I may feel too tired to get out on my own, but having Bob there with us taking charge gives me extra strength.

"I try not to compare Jonathan to other children; it is frustrating to see how much less demanding all my friends' children are. Am I doing something wrong? His needs are so strong and my mothering of him so intense that sometimes I feel as if we are from another planet. Many people cannot understand his needs and the way I respond to them. We are definitely not the average American mother and baby.

"The hidden bomb in this whole scheme of things is the taxing effect this style of parenting has on your marriage. When the child sleeps with you and goes to bed late after an energetic evening, and you have put in long days, day after day, the strain adds up immeasurably. Bob and I both had needs that were not being met. I was converted to the attachment philosophy of parenting almost overnight. Bob, however, took longer to understand why it was so important to Jonathan and me, and there was a lot of tension between us until he did. His support was very, very important to me. I needed someone to protect and defend me while I tended to our baby.

"I also felt guilty about neglecting Bob, but there was very little I could do to change the situation. I was conscious and even sympathetic of Bob's need to have some time and attention from me, but I felt as though I had nothing left over to give to him. This naturally created tension between us, but generally Bob was fairly patient and tried not to put much pressure on me, for which I was grateful. Jonathan was a daily test of our strength and commitment to each other. During the first year, Bob slept on the couch many nights, and we were like ships passing in the night. Jonathan consumed so much time and energy from both of us that we had to schedule any intimate time together."

A Note From Bob

"Overall, I feel that attachment parenting is a positive practice for our family. It is easy to see how well Jonathan responds to it. Since I was raised with a more conventional style of parenting, it took me a little time to go along with it totally. The most obvious frustration for me is a lack of intimacy with my wife. After a full day of mothering Jonathan she is too exhausted. After the close contact with Jonathan all day she seeks out time for herself—time to read, sew, get a long-postponed chore done, or just get some rest. Most of our conversations take place on the run or over the chattering of an enthusiastic two-year-old. My wife and I do enough things with Jonathan that I never really feel left out as a parent. I don't feel the need to compete against my son for Nancy's time, either. Despite my frustrations I truly believe that Jonathan's needs are more important at this time than mine. At two years of age Jonathan is not yet capable of dealing with his frustrations, but I am capable of dealing with mine.

"Jonathan has certainly developed my patience. I am often forced to display amounts of it I never knew I had—not only with Jonathan, but with Nancy, too. The mother of a fussy baby is not always the easiest person to deal with after an especially trying day. Amazingly enough, that sense of commitment toward Jonathan tended to work its way into the relationship between Nancy and me. Because we had to go to the bottom of our resources to meet Jonathan's needs, we found a new awareness and respect for each other's strengths. Nancy's willingness to set aside her own needs to nurse Jonathan wherever and whenever had a real impact on me as a father and husband. She gives me inspiration when I feel I'm giving up too much.

"I can't comfort Jonathan the way Nancy can, but at least I can be supportive of her. While Jonathan reaps the benefits of twenty-four-hour-a-day parenting, nevertheless it should come as a warning that no one can spend that amount of time with a child without experiencing some sort of impatience and frustration. At two years of age Jonathan is still a high need child. Because he enjoyed feeling right early on, any deviation from that feeling meets with immediate disapproval."

Back to Nancy

"Things eased up a bit the second year, but life with Jonathan still was not easy. He became happier with each new acquired skill. Walking and talking diffused some of his overabundant energy, and he became a bit more independent of me. He gradually became less of a 'hold me' baby, but still has spent far more time than any baby I know in my arms or on my lap. Weaning is following the same pattern. He is a comparatively frequent nurser, but I see a very gradual tapering off. I still can't help but notice the looks on other people's faces when they see us nursing. Jonathan will probably always be a very sensitive person, but over the past few months he has learned to handle his reactions to sudden sounds and sights better. He remains a very light sleeper.

"What would I say to parents with fussy babies? What do I wish I had known two years ago? Most important: Listen to your instincts and listen to your baby! I have always assumed that Jonathan cried for a reason, even if I couldn't figure out what it was. The more I followed his cues and my own feelings and observations (instead of others' advice), the easier it became to meet his needs promptly, to help him feel content, and to grow more self-confident as a mother.

"I was once told that a 'good baby' is a baby who cries and lets you know what he needs. That really puts a new perspective on fussy babies—they cry more because they need more!

"One often hears that a family should not change its routines for a new baby—the baby will have to learn to fit in. That just is not true—especially for a high need baby. For everyone's sanity, the family has to adapt to meet the needs of that baby because the baby doesn't know how to be any different. When Jonathan was born, I never dreamed that he would wind up sleeping in my bed or that I would nurse him for more than two years. Bob never expected to spend some nights on the couch, cook our breakfast, or occasionally go to a movie by himself. We had to learn to throw out our unrealistic expectations and find ways to meet everyone's needs.

"It takes a certain amount of faith to raise a demanding child. Jonathan is past two, and I often wonder if he will ever sleep through the night, learn to go to sleep without nursing, or view his potty as more than something to stand on. When doubts creep in, I have to remind myself that he learned to walk and talk on his own when he was ready even though I was afraid that because I carried him so much he would never learn to sit up! And he will probably do everything else when he is ready. In other words, if I do my best to meet his needs, he will do his best to grow up.

The Pay-Off
"I can honestly say that having a fussy baby was a blessing. I am glad I was given this type of baby. When he was six months old, I would not have been able to say this, but from the perspective of over two years, looking back at all we have given each other in our relationship, I can see tremendous benefits. Jonathan is growing into a bright, happy, adven-

turous, and most loving child. He is interested in the world around him and is willing to try almost anything as long as Mommy is right there with him. He is kind to others, gentle and loving with babies, and shows an awareness of my feelings. This probably sounds like a mother bragging, but these are all qualities that other people have remarked about. Amazingly the same people who earlier criticized our parenting style now take notice of the results.

"There are some wonderful rewards for putting all that time and energy into a difficult baby. A good example in our case is the subject of discipline. I know Jonathan inside and out and can usually tell what he is thinking. This makes discipline techniques such as verbal instruction, explanation of logical consequences, and modeling (the best of all) very effective tools for teaching him about the world and his place in it. On occasion we must correct Jonathan and dish out negative feedback, but this rarely comes in the form of spanking. Because Jonathan gets so much positive input, the slightest negative response usually does the trick.

"Jonathan is not the only one who is growing. I know I have matured in many ways by caring for him. I think I am more tolerant of other people, and I know I am far more patient and understanding. My confidence in myself not only as a mother but as a person has greatly increased. Caring for Jonathan has been the greatest effort of my life, and I am more willing now to take on challenges in other areas. I have always tended to plan too far ahead, and Jonathan has taught me the value of flexibility and concentrating on immediate concerns without too much worry towards the future. (At the same time I've learned that it pays to stay one step ahead of him to keep things as smooth as possible.) Providing Jonathan with the intense mothering he has needed has been an extremely satisfying experience for me. It has fulfilled my needs to be creative and to accomplish something tangible and worthwhile. I would never have felt this satisfaction had I left him in the care of someone else and returned to work or school.

"Jonathan has become willing to stay now and then with one of his grandmothers for up to three or four hours. I don't leave him often, but when I do, I explain that I am leaving for a little while and ask if it's all right with him. He acknowledges that he understands and that it is okay. He gives me a hug and reminds me to be back soon. I can see that there is no distress on his part when I leave or return, so that has made me more comfortable about leaving him. Waiting until Jonathan is ready to do something on his own is far more natural and enjoyable for us than an unhappy schedule of pushing him into something too early.

"I must admit that there are times when I miss being the exclusive interest in Jonathan's life, but when one of these moments arises, all I have to do is give him a big hug, and he stops what he is doing and returns it. Mostly, however, I am so proud to see Jonathan growing into a happy, loving, and self-confident little person, especially when I realize that he has done it on his own. I have simply given him the support he needed.

"Seeing the result of hard work is rewarding, of course, but experiencing the close relationship we share is the best pay-off of all. Jonathan and I have gone through a lot together and we both know it. In doing so, we have formed an unbreakable bond of love and understanding, and that is what has made it all worthwhile."

INDEX

Abdominal relaxation techniques, 89-90
Acidophilus, 93
Air swallowing
  during crying, 74-75
  during feeding, 117, 118-20
Alcohol in colic medication, 94
Allergies, 76-77, 110, 116, 122
  to cow's milk, 76-77
Anticholinergics, 94
Antiflatulents, 93, 94
Antispasmodics, 93, 94
Attachment
  behaviors that promote, 15, 17, 19-21, 25, 52, 55
  mother-infant, 12-13, 15-22, 25
  parent-infant, 3
Attachment parenting
  benefits of, 5, 39-41, 150-51, 179-89

and burnout risk, 147
and crying, 38, 59
defined, 34-36, 38-39
and father's role, 155
and self-esteem, 172

Baby
  carriages, 103
  carriers, 56, 101
  easy
    See Easy baby.
  fussy
    See Colic, Fussy baby, High need child.
"Barracuda" breastfeeding babies, 118
Baths, 104, 115
Bedtime rituals, 143
Biological rhythms, 80

Breastfeeding
  advantages
    for baby, 109-110, 120-21
    for mother, 58, 110-11
  as comforting technique, 38,
      54-55
  frequency, 20, 56, 115, 122
  and fussiness, 77-78, 80, 111-12
  to induce sleep, 14, 141, 142-43
  positioning, 113, 117
  techniques for overcoming
      difficulties, 113-16, 117-18
Burnout, 135, 145-59
  causes of, 146-49
  preventing, 150-51, 153
  risk factors, 148
  warning signs, 149
Burping, 118-20

Caffeine, 111-12
Caregiver
  responsive, 12-13, 15-16, 17, 19,
      23-24, 92-93, 180
  restrained, 20-21, 24-25, 67-68, 93
Child abuse, 67-68
Childbirth
  as a cause of fussiness, 32, 36,
      78, 81
  prepared, 34-35, 133
Colic, 71-95
  carry, 87-88
  causes of, 73-81
  cry, type of, 71-72
  dance, 86-89, 99, 100, 103
  defined, 71-73
  duration, 82-83
  evening, 72-73, 79-82
  and feeding
    breastfeeding, 110-12
    formula-feeding, 116
    solid foods, 121
    techniques, 118-19
  gas as cause, 74-75
  incidence, 83
  parent's emotional response, 73
  what to do about it, 81-82, 86-95,
      135-36
Constipation, 89-94, 122
Cortisone, 80

Cow's milk, 76-77
  causes fussiness in breastfed
      infants, 76-77, 111
"Cry it out" advice, 20-44, 60-67,
      131, 163-64, 167
Cry prints, 47
Crying, 43-68
  as communication, 46-47, 56-57,
      65, 67
  effect on listener, 52-53, 62-63,
      67-68
  frequency and duration, 49-50
  in high need babies, 4, 10-11, 17,
  physiologic effects, 63, 65
  pitch, 46
  responding to, 38, 43-44, 50-52,
      54-55, 56-60, 62, 93
  types of, 47-49
  volume, 46
Counseling, 19, 68
Cultural expectations, 22, 79

Dancing, 31, 86-89, 99-100
Darwin, Charles, 45-46
Delayed fusser, 16-17, 40, 53, 79
Demands, high need baby's, 4, 17,
      23
Dependence, 125
Development, infant, 21, 40, 65,
      168, 182-83
Diaper rash, 86, 110
Diary, 31, 84-85
Dicyclomine, 93
Discipline, 63, 171-78, 188-89

Ear infections, 85-86
Easy baby, 15-17, 22, 53, 181
Edison, Thomas, 46
Engorgement, 117

Fathers, 39, 85, 127-37, 180
  comforting baby, 100, 102-3,
      135-36
  and mothering the mother,
      133-35, 153-56
  prenatal involvement, 31, 33, 133
  and sexuality, 130

Feeding, 5, 48, 56, 109-23
  See also Breastfeeding, Formula
    feeding.
Fetus, research on, 28-33
Food intolerance, 77-78
Formula
  feeding, 61, 76, 116-17, 121
  predigested, 76, 116-17
  soy, 76, 116
Freeway therapy, 102-3, 136
Fussy baby
  case history, 191-202
  causes of, 7-11, 14, 16-17, 29,
    32-33, 36, 73-81
  defined, 2-5, 22-23
  effect on parent, 52-53, 128-29,
    147, 151
  fathering, 127-37
  feeding, 109-23
  how to comfort, 86-93, 97-108,
    135-36, 141-44
  personality as older child, 180-81
  and shutdown, 161-69
  sleep probems, 139-41
  weaning, 123-25

Gardener, William, 16
Gassiness, 74-75, 77, 89-90, 112
Glycerin suppository, 89, 94
Goodness of fit concept, 8-9, 24,
    128
Grief, 168
Growth hormone, 80
Guilt, maternal, 50-51, 58-59, 65, 67

High need baby
  benefits of attachment parenting
    for, 182-86
  after birth, 53-55
  and child abuse, 67-68
  as a colicky baby, 78-79
  defined, 2-6
  and discipline, 171-78
  how to comfort, 86-93, 97-108,
    135-36, 141-44
  and parenting styles, 17-21, 24

  shutdown, 161-69
  sleep problems, 140-41
  weaning, 123-25
High need children
  and discipline, 172-78
  and junk food, 123
Hormones
  baby's as cause of colic, 80-81
  maternal, 39, 50, 80, 128, 130
  stress, 29
Hospital nurseries, 54-55
Housework, 81, 130, 133, 156
Human milk, 20
  substances in, 77-78, 111-12
  taste, changes in, 77-78, 112
Hyperactive children, 185
Hypertonic babies, 5, 105, 113-14

Independence, 125, 183
Intelligence, 23-25
Interaction counseling, 19
Intuition
  father's, 34, 50, 137
  mother's, 17, 34, 50, 57, 65

Junk food, 123

Kramer vs. Kramer, 150

La Leche League, 35, 125
Lactose intolerance, 110
Lambskin, 105
Laying on of hands, 31
Let-down, 115-16, 117

Marathon nursing, 115
Marriage, 35, 130, 133, 137, 155-57
Marsupial mothering, 102
Massage, infant, 89-90, 91, 105, 114
Medication for colic, 93-94
Milk ejection reflex, 115-16, 117
Modeling, 184, 189

Mother
    anxious, 75
    attachment to baby, 12-13, 15-22,
        128-29
    benefits of breastfeeding for,
        110-11
    burnout, 145-59
    diet while breastfeeding, 77-78,
        111-12
    emotions affect unborn baby,
        29-35
    hormonal responses
        See Hormones, maternal.
    as housekeeper, 130-31
    intuition
        See Intuition, mother's.
    needs, 133-35, 157-58
    as organizer of baby's behavior,
        13, 22
    response to infant cry, 50-53,
        56-59, 65-68, 131
    responsive, 15-17
    restrained, 20-22
    Supermom myth, 146
Music, 29-31, 107

Naps, 82
Nature vs. nurture, 8
Need level concept, 10-11, 34, 128
Needs, unfilled, 11
Nestle nursing, 142
New York Longitudinal Study,
    180-81

Obesity, 120-21
Organization, baby's after birth,
    8-10, 13-14

Pacifier, 91-92
Physical contact with baby, as
    soothing technique, 4, 56, 58,
    86-87, 110
Physician, communicating with,
    83-84
Postpartum, 27, 53-55
Pregnancy, 27, 28-33, 150
Progesterone and colic, 80-81

Prolactin, 39, 57-58, 80, 110, 123,
    143, 151
    and smoking, 78
Prostaglandins, 81
Punishment, 171, 175-76, 177-78

Rhythms, biological, 80
Rocking, 99, 100, 141
Rooming-in, 36, 54, 55

Schedules, 56, 61
Separation from mother, 3, 14, 20,
    161-67
Self-esteem, 23-24, 172, 186
Self-soothing, 14, 22, 65
Sensitivity of high need babies, 2,
    9
Sexual drive, 130
Shutdown syndrome, 161-69
Simethicone, 93
Sleep
    cycles, 140-41, 142
    patterns, 14, 38
    position, 90
    problems, 5, 14, 22, 139-41,
        158-59
    sharing, 38, 142, 180
Smoking, 78
Solid foods, 121-23
    readiness for, 122
Songs, 29-31
Soothing techniques, 81-82, 97-108,
    135-36
Spanking, 177-78
Spoiling, 59-60, 62-63, 183
Stimulus barrier, 9, 140
Stress, 25, 29, 32
    factors leading to burnout, 148
Strollers, 103
Sucking, 5, 91
Swings, 102

Tantrums, 173-74, 176
Tape recordings of infant cries, 84,
    107
Tea, herbal, 94

Mc ___ ___ 469-3773
455-7730 / Robin 815-485-8830

LA LECHE LEAGUE MEMBERSHIP

As you read through the pages of this book, you'll notice several references to La Leche League. La Leche League was founded in 1956 by seven women who had learned about successful breastfeeding while nursing their own babies. They wanted to share this information with other mothers. Now over 9,000 League Leaders and 3,500 League Groups carry on that legacy. League Leaders are always willing to answer questions about breastfeeding and mothering and are available by phone for help with breastfeeding problems. League Groups meet monthly in communities all over the world to share breastfeeding information and mothering experiences.

When you join LLL, you participate in an international mother-to-mother helping network, a valuable resource for parenting help and support. Your annual membership fee of $20.00 brings you six bimonthly issues of NEW BEGINNINGS, a magazine filled with stories, hints, and inspiration from other breastfeeding families. Members receive our LLLI Catalogues by mail and they are entitled to a 10% discount on purchases from LLLI's wide variety of outstanding books and publications on breastfeeding, childbirth, nutrition, and parenting.

Why should you join La Leche League? Because you care—about your own family and about mothers and babies all over the world!

Return this form to La Leche League International,
P. O. Box 1209, Franklin Park, IL 60131-8209 USA.

_____ I'd like to join La Leche League International. Enclosed is my annual membership fee of $20.

_____ In addition, I am enclosing a tax-deductible donation of $_____ to support the work of La Leche League.

_____ Please send me a copy of THE WOMANLY ART OF BREASTFEEDING, softcover, $7.95 plus $1.50 for shipping and handling. *(In California and Illinois, please add sales tax.)*

_____ Please send me La Leche League's FREE Catalogue

_____ Please send me a FREE copy of the Directory of LLL representatives. *(Please enclose a self-addressed, stamped envelope.)*

_____
Name

_____
Address

_____
State/Province   *Zip/Postal Code*   *Country*

Temperament
 baby's, 2, 7, 8-11, 15-23, 35, 78,
  89, 177, 185
 mother's, 15-22, 75, 151
Tennyson, Alfred Lord, 45
Tense mother/tense baby syndrome,
  75
Thumb-sucking, 14
Tonic bite, 114
Trampoline, 103
Trust, 24, 62, 66, 173, 176, 186

Uncuddly baby, 4-5, 18, 19
Urinary tract infections, 86

Verny, Thomas, 30
Vestibular system, 14, 98-99
Vocal cords, 46

Warm fuzzy, 87-88, 104-5
Waterbed, 105
Weaning, 38, 123-25
White noise, 107
Womb environment, 8-10, 13, 28-33,
  97-98